GROWING
CONSCIOUSNESS

GROWING
CONSCIOUSNESS

THE GARDENER'S GUIDE TO SEEDING THE SOUL

LEO CARVER

MANDALA

SAN RAFAEL • LOS ANGELES • LONDON

⇶ CONTENTS ⇷

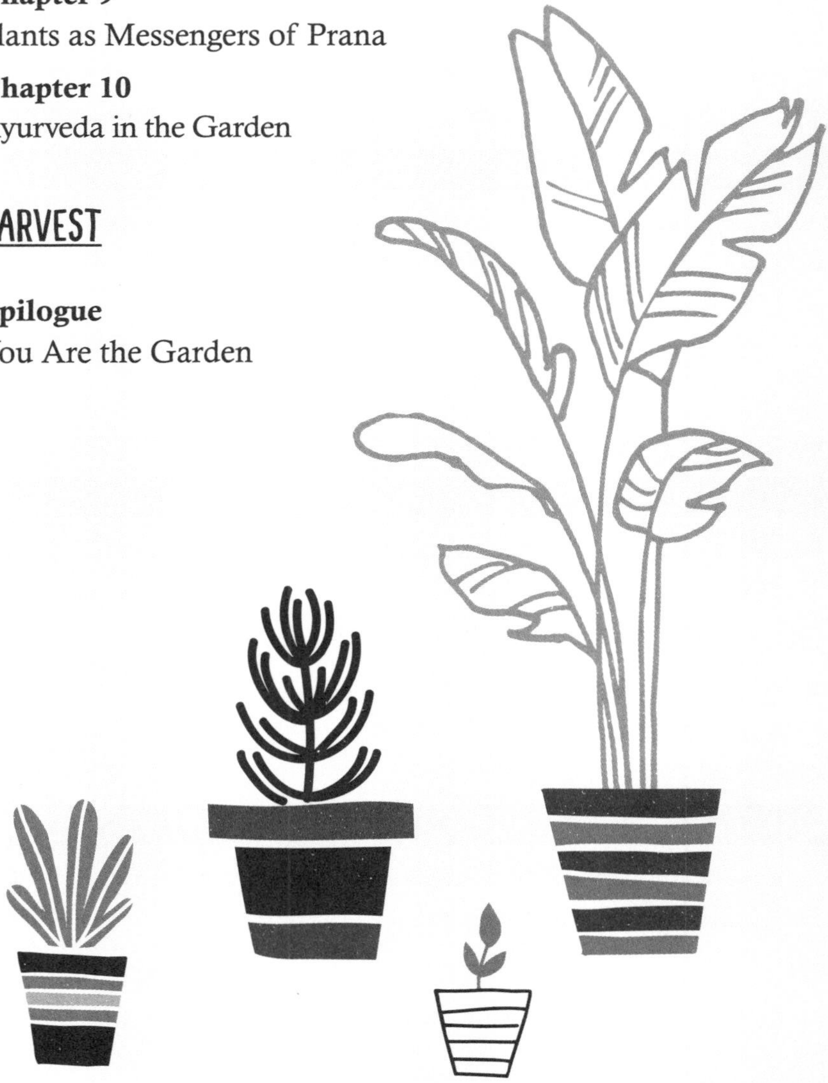

FOREWORD

Growing up in a traditional Hindu Rig Vedic Brahmin family with an extensive Ayurvedic background, being grateful of nature was almost ingrained in my psyche. My parents would have me sit in our front yard on a chair in the middle of the home garden and ask me to be silent and listen to the wind, the birds, or to breathe in the fragrance of the jasmine flowers, the aroma from the kitchen—anything in the environment—just notice, they would say. I didn't know then that I was learning a valuable skill that would help me become a more balanced individual in my adult life. My parents essentially taught me to appreciate nature, to be grateful for it, to become one with nature, and become more conscious of my actions

At this point in time, becoming a disease-free society is the high ideal that I want to help achieve. And so does Leo. The steps towards achieving this goal begin with raising our collective consciousness. The bottom-line is, when we intentionally or unintentionally violate the laws of nature, there cannot be perfect health.

Following the laws of nature is crucial in order to lead a healthy, balanced life. Ayurveda emphasizes the need for balance and harmony in life with help from nature itself. This dynamic balance needs to be achieved in all aspects of a person's life: physical, chemical, intellectual, emotional, behavioral, spiritual, social, and universal. Growing your consciousness is key. Once you silence your mind, you allow the environment to talk to you.

This book provides you the tools you need to meditate and open yourself up to receiving a different perception.

Mythological stories and historical evidence show that gardens have had a depth of spirituality for humankind. From the Garden of Eden to Hanging Gardens of Babylon, to the Rishis who sat under Kalpavruksha and meditated for days on end to achieve enlightenment, humans have had a deep-seated connection with nature. Not just with the fruits, flowers, and food that gardens bear us but from the time that it all begins from the SEED.

"Water the root to enjoy the fruit" is something that Maharishi Mahesh Yogi used to say in relation to all aspects of life—from birth to business, from health to wealth. It simply means you need to put your intentions in the right area to let them sprout. Watering the roots is about putting your intentions in the right place which allows them to manifest when it is time—just like a tree bears fruit when the season is perfect. Another simple mantra to live by is "Where attention goes, energy flows" which is indicative of how scattered our lives have become. Allowing yourself the ability to focus on a specific task at hand or even a simple thought, gives rise to the possibility of manifesting your desires!

According to Ayurveda, the human body is like an upside-down tree. It has its roots at the top and the branches below. When we say that the body, the mind, and the spirit are connected, all it means is that there is hope for our individual self to connect with our cosmic self, if only we explore our preexisting **connection** with mother nature. Our individual self stems from our thoughts that turn into actions. A repeated action becomes a habit and a series of habits performed every day is a routine and eventually your lifestyle. Being in nature helps us become more mindful and aware of our emotions and possibilities. That's the reason--forest bathing, spending time in nature heals the very core aspect of our Prana-- which is the life force.

Even traditional science has now proved that spending time in green spaces and sunlight can boost serotonin levels in the body and hence improve the overall happiness. In a study of about 20,000 people, found that the ones who spent 120 minutes a week in nature— local parks or other natural environments—reported good health and psychological well-being than the ones who did not spend time in nature!

In the late 1940s, a Romanian doctor, Franz Halberg, started tracking the levels of circulating white blood cells in mice. He noticed that the WBC count was the highest during the day and fell at night. Even though he observed different strains of mice had different WBC counts, every type of mouse had a sharp rise during the day and a similar fall at night.

He went on to track hourly changes in blood pressure, heart rates of mice, and body temperature. He found that similar to the WBC count, these physiological responses also follow a similar 24-hour schedule. Thus, the term "circadian rhythm" was coined and Halberg went on to prove that humans also follow a similar predictable schedule based on an internal clock that was light-dependent!

What does this mean for us in the 21st century? As human beings, we are a part of nature and we are physiologically governed by nature's laws. It is precisely why our body clocks are attuned to waking up with the sunrise and unwinding at nightfall. In the era of being surrounded with screens, our bodies defy nature's laws and give in to the vicious cycle of sleeping late and being exhausted in the morning. Spending time in nature, keeping your body active, and eating according to your dosha type can help restore the balance and consciously live a healthier life.

FOREWORD

My favorite way of growing consciousness is through nutrition. That's right—we all need to eat! Nutrition doesn't have to be all that expensive. And it can absolutely be natural, organic, and fresh from your backyard! And that's why investing time and energy in your own garden can work wonders for your health. That's also one of the many reasons why this book strikes a chord with me. It dives deep into the scientific significance of using plants and herbs of the garden for nutrition and establishes the spiritual connection of the mind, the body, and the garden. Through this book you can actually start your own Ayurvedic garden and bring a higher level of consciousness to your food choices. It is not only about medicine but also about wellness.

The Vedas heralded meditating in nature as a pathway to attaining higher levels of consciousness thousands of years ago. Recently, scientific studies have proven the efficacy of meditation on alleviating stress, anxiety, and trauma symptoms. This book shows you how you can tap into your relationship with your garden and learn about your true Self. You'll be able to recognize that your act of gardening is all about interacting with living beings. You'll bring a higher level of consciousness into the act of gardening and extend the same love and care with which you'd tend to the needs of any other human or animal.

Meditating unlocks your ability to listen, ability to talk. Ability to think. You can listen to your body. Listen to the beat of your heart. Listen to what your gut is trying to tell you.

When you're one with nature, you're already on your way to becoming one with your true Self. You can talk to yourself and engage in thoughts that you would normally not be able to think at your usual level of consciousness. You can identify your purpose, unlock your hidden potential and live your best life.

DR. MANAS KSHIRSAGAR

SEEDS OF CONSCIOUSNESS

"Life begins the day you start a garden."
—*Chinese proverb*

Every moment of life is a seed. Every seed is an expression of life's pure potential. As an example, we can simply look at the present moment. There was a seed of consciousness, an idea, that led to you holding this book, to reading these words. Something has brought you to this very place, and that mysterious something is its own kind of seed.

Normally, when we refer to a seed, it is thought of as an embryonic plant to be sown in the ground, or in mammals as semen seeking the fruitful womb. Always, the seed is the potential start. But did you know seeds exist in nonphysical ways as well? Seeds can be moments of intention and awareness. Seeds can be planted in times of clarity or connection with others. Mental and spiritual growth comes from these nonphysical seeds all the time, giving life to the very impactful experience of our thoughts and emotions.

Since the beginning of humankind, we have searched for the origin of our existence. Some may call it God, or the Divine Source, and some attribute the beginning of this reality to a Big Bang cosmic event, while others may not bother to even ask the question. However, it is undeniable that something seeded our universe, and that creative act has led to this very moment and will continue in this way. Life in perpetual expression. It can be agreed that a seed contains infinite potential—potential for any possibility once it has found fertile soil and favorable conditions for life. This potential exists long before any action is taken, held within the seed body, waiting and ready to be unlocked.

Your interest in spiritual gardening connects us on a journey toward unlocked potential. It is essentially the seed of the experiences you will gain through what is shared here. It is the source of the expanded awareness of ourselves and our gardens that we are growing into. We can gain personal insight about the nature of a seed when thought of in this way. Although this work is focused on gardening, it is written to help you see beyond the actions involved and to connect with it on a higher level—in essence, to learn the art of gardening your soul and tending to your spirit.

We will approach your consciousness as a seed and provide it with the elements that it needs to grow. Your garden will come to be more than just a plot of land, or a few pots or raised beds. You will know how your garden can connect you to life more fully. In doing so, it will also take on more significance as a place of nourishment spiritually, mentally, and physically.

By the end of this book, you will be equipped to be not only a more mindful gardener of plants but also a more skilled harvester of the gifts of your own being. Peace, calm, insight, balance, serenity, connection, clarity, love, and gratitude can all be grown and brought into your life just as skillfully as you grow green beans, tomatoes, or corn. This holistic approach to the garden bears many fruits. Let's learn and garden together, for as we garden, we will not only grow food, but, most importantly, we will also grow our own consciousness.

Every moment of life is a seed, and the present moment is always the start of what is to come. We will make use of meditation and mindfulness to get better acquainted with the present moment. In cultivating greater present-moment awareness, we will plant the seed from which our life may bloom. This is the beginning of how we heighten our gardening experience; this is how we use it to grow consciousness.

BASICS OF MEDITATION

Let's take some time to get clear and centered. This will provide the right mental and spiritual backdrop for soaking up the information and intentions of this book. You may be new to meditation, but as you'll see, it is a valuable tool. For our purposes, meditation will mainly serve as a way of calibrating our mind-set and energy. Throughout this book, you will find written guided meditations as exercises to help bring together the chapters and their messages into an experience. If you are not familiar with meditation, here are a few things to note:

- There is no true wrong way to meditate. You will experience one of four scenarios, and, believe it or not, none of them is a waste of your time. You will either:
    - fall asleep;
    - stay in silence but feel as if nothing is happening;
    - go on a mental ride, distracted by your thoughts and emotions; or
    - relax into a peaceful experience.
- Meditation is all about you! There is no competition or comparison to be made with others. There is no such thing as someone meditating better than you. So, let go of any thoughts of others.
- Be comfortable. Do not feel as if you must sit in a particular position. Certain postures have been scientifically developed over centuries of meditation practice and doctrine, so they definitely have their purposes. However, they are not the main focus of meditation.

If sitting cross-legged is not comfortable for you, sit in a chair or with your legs in a more comfortable position. Relaxation is a very important factor to a meditative experience. So, be comfortable, even if this means lying down. Just be aware that our goal in meditation is not to sleep, but to experience our inner world with awareness and attention. If you fall asleep, it doesn't negate the meditation, but, ultimately, that is not your aim.

● Do your best to let go of your attachment to your thoughts and emotions. This may seem difficult at first if you are not accustomed. But don't worry; just allow the thoughts to come and go. Meditation is about observation, relaxation, and openness. Your mind may try to work through nagging thoughts or occurrences, it may use this as an opportunity to figure something out, or the mind may present you with underlying background baggage that you weren't aware of. None of this is bad, but you don't want to let it distract you from the simple awareness of your own presence.

● There are many ways to meditate; however, they all are intended to bring you to a place of self-awareness, clarity, and peacefulness. One cannot accomplish this by going along with the never-ending cascade of thoughts pouring into the mind. So, be still in body and mind. Simply observe without attachment, not giving any thought your attention. Instead, treat thoughts like clouds floating in a big, open sky, while keeping your focus on the panoramic view that is your inner world.

As stated, meditations have been placed throughout the book to correspond with the information you are receiving. If they are followed with genuine openness and receptivity, they can accomplish their intended goal of bringing you more in tune with the material. Especially for beginning meditators, your first pass at the exercise may not seem to yield any noticeable results. However, they are intended to be revisited, and it is recommended that you come back to the meditations whenever it suits you.

For best results, read through the entire exercise once and then actually go into meditation. This will allow your mind to release the how of the practice and simply be present. This is a good way to not think so much about it. Even if you just skim through the exercise, it will be beneficial to know the steps involved beforehand rather than reading and trying it as you go.

Once you are familiar with the meditation, try pulling it back out during your growing season. If you feel inspired by something like pleasant weather, or the growth of your garden, during this time, consider pairing an appropriate meditation from the book with your experience. This will only further amplify the effects of the experience. Another tip is to either record yourself reading the exercise or have someone else read it to you. This way, you can just listen and not think about the process. Recording yourself and listening to the recorded meditation tends to add extra depth to the meaning of the words and may prove most efficient for some. Either way, don't overthink it.

Now that we have gone over some of the basics of meditation, let's try it out. Since this is the beginning of our exploration, we will start with a meditation intended to seed your consciousness with harmony and receptivity toward the information you are about to process.

⪢⪢⪢ SOUL-SEEDING MEDITATION ⪡⪡⪡

Let's begin by finding a comfortable seated position. As stated earlier, you can lie down, or sit on the ground or a chair—whatever is most comfortable for you. Once you are settled, close your eyes. Keep your eyes closed and sit as still as possible. Focus your attention on your breath. Begin by pushing out as much air as you can without strain, gently squeezing your diaphragm with the intention of emptying yourself completely—mentally and physically. On your next inhalation, relax your diaphragm as if you were letting the air flow into your body rather than forcefully pulling it in.

This may take a little practice, so give yourself three or four of these deep belly breaths. Do not make it a task. If it becomes too distracting, simply watch your breathing with full attention: Visualize the air as it enters through your nose, circulates through your body, and makes its way back up and out through the nose. If you are making these into deep belly breaths, try exhaling out with gentle force, allowing the inhale to flow in slowly. Receive the inhalation with gratitude, and release the exhalation as an offering. Do this for a few moments, seven or so breaths, and relax into simple observation.

You will notice your mind's activity. It may be relatively quiet with a feeling of impatience, or it could be violently overactive, unaccustomed to this stillness. It can also be completely peaceful. Let's release our minds and focus attention on tranquility. Take a few more deep breaths in this way, noticing the calm as it washes over your body. It may help to mentally scan yourself as you breathe, starting with the top of your head and relaxing more and more with each breath, down your body, until you reach the soles of your feet. If needed, repeat this step a couple of times until you have reached a noticeable point of relaxation.

Now, consider your intentions for reading and learning about this topic. What are your goals? If you want to deepen your gardening experience, silently ask yourself this within. If you want to learn more about yourself and connect with Nature, allow this intention to flow out of your heart. Whatever your reasons are, be in the present and acknowledge that those intentions were the seed of this very moment. Remember the first time you became aware of this book, or the first time you thought about gardening as more than just agriculture. Think of your interest in herbs or food in general. Something has brought you here. Remain still and allow your heart to reveal what that something is. Keep your eyes closed and your awareness on the breath. As your mind presents you with thoughts, simply witness. Let it tell you what it will, but do not engage with the thoughts. Breathe deeply and observe. By now, you should feel relaxed into the experience, but if you find that your mind is still restless, just return to watching your breathing.

Now, visualize a vibrant, lush bush in front of you. Let your imagination paint the visual with beautiful green leaves and colorful flowers. See the healthy stalk and roots of the plant. Feel its aliveness. If your imagination will take the visual only so far, that is fine. Don't make it a chore. This is not about doing, but about feeling and allowing. If your imagination adds to the visual with movement or other features, this is also OK. Just be with this wonderful plant and hold its vision in your mind. Next, see the plant reverse through its life cycle. Watch it shrink back into a sapling and then to a sprout. Watch the sprout collapse back down into a seed.

Now, while holding your silence and stillness, imagine this seed floating before you. Pay attention to whatever details of the seed your mind will allow. See its curvature and shape. Notice the indentions and color of it. Make it as real in your mind as you can without distracting yourself. Hold this image for three or four breath cycles. On the next inhalation, picture this seed entering your body and resting at your heart. Visualize the seed settling into place with a green glow. If it helps, place your hand on your chest. Focus your attention on this seed and feel your body's energy. Spend a few moments like this, not thinking about anything else. Just feel your own presence and the energy that you have invited in.

Now, before we close this meditation, silently speak through your heart to this imaginary seed. Hold the vision and say, "Thank you for coming into my life. In me, you will grow." Repeat this statement inwardly as you breathe in five more deep breaths: "Thank you for coming into my life. In me, you will grow." After the five breaths are complete, release the visual. Relax your control on your breath and let it flow naturally. When you are ready, slowly open your eyes.

CHAPTER 1

THE SPIRIT THAT MOVES THROUGH THE GARDEN

"The Lord God took the man and put him in the
Garden of Eden to work it and keep it."

—*Genesis 2:15*

Throughout history, gardens have held a special place for human
beings. Prior to the cultivation of the soil, it is thought, people were
hunter-gatherers and foragers. Yet anthropological evidence suggests
that even in those times, prehistoric individuals maintained their own
forest gardens, making use of areas where edible plants were found
in abundance. These early gardens were probably little more than
frequently visited and protected plots of land where humanity slowly
developed its gardening skill.

Researchers in the Amazon have proposed that the Maya were
farming far back into antiquity, based on the unnatural distribution of certain plants within the region that were known to be

used for food and medicine. While this wouldn't have been the kind of gardening we think of today, the transfer and maintenance of certain favorable plants over others for human use is definitely a form of gardening.[1]

Additionally, we can look to ancient architecture to understand how long people have been engaging with the plant world. Thankfully, history has provided us with some clues as to when people started creating home gardens. Some of the earliest outdoor enclosures that could be attributed to farming and gardening appear around 12,000 years ago, during the Neolithic Age, as humanity started to settle into stationary homes.[2] In fact, many archaeologists suggest that the cultivation of plant life was the catalyst for human beings to move away from hunter-gatherer societies in the first place. As we will see, there is a long historical relationship between humans and gardening.

In ancient Kemet (what is now Egypt), there is evidence that organized agriculture was being performed as far back as 6,000 years ago. The walls of tombs, stelae, and other hieroglyphic evidence display detailed farming operations and botanical gardens from time immemorial. Many of these depictions showcase people performing agricultural tasks we still undertake today. Harvesting grain, planting fruit-bearing trees, and sowing seed are all shown on carvings from many centuries ago. If anything, it tells us that our societal development has included farming and gardening for a minimum of thousands of years.[3] So, as we seek to enhance our modern gardening practice, know that you are participating in one of the oldest known human activities. Indeed, our history is literally intertwined with the development of gardening.

---

1 Scott L. Fedick, "The Maya Forest: Destroyed or Cultivated by the Ancient Maya?" *Proceedings of the National Academy of Sciences of the United States of America* 107, no. 3 (2010), 953–954.
2 Pier Vittorio Aureli and Maria Giudici, "Gardeners' World: A Short History of Domestication and Nurturance," *Architectural Review*, January 20, 2021, https://www.architectural-review.com/essays/ecology/gardeners-world
3 "Ancient African Civilizations," Ancient Civilizations World, January 12, 2017, https://ancientcivilizationsworld.com/africa.

This spiritual bond is evident in the numerous references to gardening and the use of plants in our surviving religious texts. Societies of the past left us writings and architecture that show a common human concept of connection between the spiritual and the natural worlds.

In modern Western society, we don't have to look any further than the Bible. Its first references to humanity, like the quote at the beginning of this chapter, show humankind working and living in the Garden of Eden. In fact, numerous gardening metaphors appear throughout the Bible, from the Old Testament to the New Testament. For example, in the Book of Jeremiah, one reads, "They shall come and sing aloud on the height of Zion, and they shall be radiant over the goodness of the Lord . . . their life shall be like a watered garden, and they shall languish no more."[4] In the poetic work the Song of Solomon, the beloved says to her lover, "Blow upon my garden, let its spices flow. Let my beloved come to his garden and eat its choicest fruits."[5]

The appearance of references like these indicate that agriculture was a familiar part of life for the people of the Old Testament. Could it be that the writers of the Bible made these garden references to enhance the impact that this timeless wisdom would have on the people? To make this knowledge more digestible and accessible to everybody? Maybe by mentioning herbs and plants, these writers knew that their wisdom would not only be heard but would also one day be more likely to bear fruit.

We can also deduce that Jesus Christ was a lover of gardens, as he seems to have spent a lot of his reflective time in them and frequently used allegories from the garden. Some of his most famous teachings indicate an understanding of gardening and husbandry. Examples of this are the parable of the sower and the seed, in which he uses seed sowing to explain the public reception of his message. Here, Jesus uses simple gardening wisdom to explain his message,

---

4 Biblica, Jer. 31:12, The Bible (New International Version), https://www.biblica.com/bible.
5 Biblica, Song of Sol. 4:16.

stating, "The seed falling on rocky ground refers to someone who hears the word and at once receives it with joy. But since they have no root, they last only a short time."[6] Or consider how he teaches about faith, saying, "It is like a mustard seed, which is the smallest of all seeds on earth. Yet when planted, it grows and becomes the largest of all garden plants, with such big branches that the birds can perch in its shade."[7]

In the Book of John, Jesus is quoted as saying, "I am the vine; you are the branches. Whoever abides in me and I in him, he it is that bears much fruit, for apart from me you can do nothing."[8] This is not to mention the significance of his last moments as a free man being spent in prayer in the garden of Gethsemane, which was known to be a favorite space of retreat for him when in the region.

These are the words and actions of a man who was familiar with nature and horticulture. Jesus was able to convey profound wisdom from the garden that has touched the world up to the present day. Could there be a significance or some power in connecting these two parts of the human experience? Was Jesus' use of these garden metaphors trivial? Maybe there is a reason gardens and plants have often served as great teaching tools for the expansion of consciousness.

We can look at other references to the garden from different cultures in other parts of the world. We have already spoken of the ancient Egyptian love of gardens and agriculture. The famous excavation of Tutankhamun's tomb revealed remnants of an elaborate floral offering to the deceased king. These kinds of ritual offerings were common for both honored dead and deities of the great society. Their theocratic culture was deeply spiritual, and this understanding permeated all activities, making it among the first that we know of to draw such strong connections between consciousness and nature.

In some cases, the divine personalities of a culture were directly associated with their most honored local plants. As Linda Farrar, author of *Gardens and Gardeners of the Ancient World*, points out, "In

---

6 Biblica, Matt. 13:20–21.
7 Biblica, Mark 4:31–32.
8 Biblica, John 15:5.

each ancient culture we find a variety of deities responsible for fertility and agriculture, including specific ones intended to protect plants and crops."[9] Could this ancient practice of assigning spiritual significance to plants and nature have just been arbitrary?

The ancient Greek culture stands out among others for this practice, as we have several surviving tales of connection between the divine and the plant kingdom. Like other early civilizations, the Greek people were hardly religious by today's standards. However, their spiritual systems served as their way of connecting to and understanding the mysteries of the soul. As a result, their society made liberal use of mythology and folklore to show how the forces of nature affected our existence.

Take the story of Minthe, from which the well-known plant family mint gets its name. In this example, Hades, the god of death, has a love affair with a magical nymph, Minthe, which leads to his wife, Persephone, turning her into a plant, forever separated from death, cut down, and trampled on. As we know, human use of mint is greatly beneficial and healthy for a number of ailments and diseases, ultimately "separating" us from death. This story was the Greeks' way of explaining the healing qualities of the plant. Also, Hades, despite being unable to break the spell, gave Minthe a sweet smell so that even when trampled on, she would grace the person with sweetness and pleasure. This was an explanation for one of mint's most noticeable and attractive qualities—its unique smell. Knowing about the qualities of mint, even if through allegory, would be valuable information in early human society and still is. This simple story was a way of making mint easier to distinguish in the wild and use for medicine.[10]

Another noteworthy Greek tale is that of Apollo, Eros, and Daphne. Similar to the subject of our previous tale, Daphne was a beautiful nymph who caught the attention of an Olympian god.

9 Linda Farrar, "A Guide to Ancient Gardening," HistoryExtra, 2016, https://www.historyextra.com/period/ancient-egypt/a-guide-to-ancient-gardening.
10 Mike Greenburg, "The Naiad Minthe in Greek Mythology," Greek Myths and Legends, https://www.greeklegendsandmyths.com/minthe.html.

In this story, Apollo insults Eros and his archery skills, which leads to an angry Eros shooting him with one of his love arrows. Apollo is immediately smitten with love and lust for Daphne. In some versions of this story, she has pledged to remain a virgin, while in others Eros also shot her with an arrow that made her uninterested in Apollo's advances. Regardless, she flees from Apollo as he pursues her throughout the wild countryside and forest. Once he finally catches her, Daphne prays to her father, Peneus the river god, for help in escaping Apollo's lust. As a solution to her problem, Peneus turns Daphne into the laurel tree.

From then on, the laurel was considered sacred to Apollo and his devotees, as it was the only remaining connection he had to his first love, Daphne.[11] Greeks held this plant in high esteem, as did the Romans later, because of its importance to one of their chief gods. The laurel tree is also known as bay laurel, and it is where we get the common culinary herb bay leaf. This herb was venerated by the Greeks and Romans, being used in virtually any religious ceremony dedicated to Apollo and prized for its medicinal uses. Much like the tale of Minthe, this story correlates these health benefits with certain features of the plant as a way of teaching people about its value. Greek mythology is littered with this kind of allegorical wisdom about herbal medicine. Additionally, it shows that the people of ancient Greece understood that there is consciousness, or spirit, within the natural world. As we will see, this has been a common sentiment throughout human history.

In far eastern Asia, we find the Zen garden design, influenced by China but popularized in Japan. These gardens were influenced by Zen Buddhism and created with the intention of inspiring long periods of meditation. These were not typical gardens, filling a need for food or medicine; instead, they had primarily aesthetic value. As a result, one of the most relevant aspects of the Zen garden is its

11 Mike Greenburg, "Daphne: The Nymph of the Laurel Tree," Mythology Source, https://mythologysource.com/daphne-greek-nymph.

emphasis on incorporating primary aspects of the natural environment. Zen gardens are distinguished by their use of stone, carefully raked sand areas, skillfully trimmed shrubs, and pebble rock paths. Some may also contain other recognizable features, such as an area where herbs are cultivated or a space for flowers, but all will have those uniquely Zen effects.

The meticulous attention to detail and concentration involved in creating and maintaining a Zen garden is inspiring. Even more so, their magnificence shows in this awareness of nature. Most of the belief systems of the Far East placed a lot of spiritual significance on understanding and using the elements. Even though Eastern cultures were not alone in recognizing this, they were unique in their perspective and use of this knowledge. They regarded these elements to be metal, wood, earth, fire, and water and represented each of them in their garden.

The Japanese and Chinese are notable among the ancient cultures of the world because there was a significant focus on marrying the artificial aspects of the garden with its natural aesthetic.[12] Therefore, these cultures display a longstanding knowledge and conceptualization of the spiritual correlations of gardening. In fact, Japan produced *Sakuteiki* (translation: *Records of Garden Making*), arguably the world's oldest written guide on garden design. In this book, many styles are available to enhance the Zen concept of meditation. This kind of detail and attention indicates a deep understanding of how the human spirit can be nurtured through nature and how this can be captured and encouraged through our gardens.

For instance, the requirements of maintaining a pristine space in this way necessitates that the gardener cultivate focus and patience like very few other activities can. That alone can produce other mental and spiritual gifts.

---

12 Ignacio Aristimuño, "History of Japanese Gardens," Japan Visitor, https://www.japanvisitor.com/japanese-culture/history-japanese-gardens.

Another benefit of practicing this gardening style is balance. Time spent in nature can be a valuable counter to the business of worldly affairs, providing space for free thinking and clarity. The fact that these gardens are created specifically for that purpose makes the healing qualities that much more potent. The whole concept of Zen gardens is very much aligned with the intentions of this book, providing historical context and credibility to this spiritual way of gardening. Although these Asian masterpieces were usually not intended for their produce, they do show an ancient cultural desire for exploring the spiritual side of communing with our plants.

Aside from spiritually inspired garden designs, it should also be noted that we get the philosophy of Shintoism from the Far East. Shinto, considered a nature religion, is most likely the oldest form of spirituality to be found in Japan.[13] Like other belief systems from around the world, it is centered on the idea that consciousness is present and accessible to humanity through plants and the natural elements. Shinto philosophy teaches that the natural forces of the land, forests, and mountains are imbued with power that can help people and guide them in their troubles. These *kami*, or sacred powers, could be approached and appeased as if they were conscious. In fact, it is thought that the first Shinto shrines were probably created for agricultural reasons—that is, to pray for better crops and for rain, and for environmental concerns. As we will see, this is a common conceptualization of how humans can reach the higher dimensions of our spiritual experience.

In West Africa and central Africa, we also see the ideation of the natural world as imbued with consciousness, power, and information. Traditional religions such as voodoo and those of the Yoruba, the Akan, the Dogon, the Ewe, the Berber, the Dinka, and the Maasai, among many others, all have similar reverence for nature. This is seen in the way practitioners perform rituals outdoors, make use of herbal medicine, and seek communion with the environmental forces. Each

---

13 Joseph M. Kitagawa, *On Understanding Japanese Religion* (Princeton, NJ: Princeton University Press, 1987).

of these belief systems teaches that the divine creator of all things, their principal deity, acts through nature and has delegated the functioning of life on Earth through the intelligences of the elements and other aspects of the world—thunder, animals, or sacred spaces.

While various peoples may all call these forces by different names, the basic principles in all of them correlate. An example of this is the archetypal energy of the mother goddess. Because of the differences in terrain and the qualities of the environment, this mother deity may be associated with different natural forces in different parts of the continent. However, her basic qualities of motherhood, fertility, rain, water of some sort, and bountiful harvest always follow. In Yorubaland (West Africa), this energy may be associated with the names Yemoja or Oshun, while in South Africa, the Zulu called her Mbaba Mwana Waresa. In what is now Benin, formerly the Kingdom of Dahomey, the Fon called her Gleti, and the ancient Egyptians and Nubians may have attached this energy to Auset (Isis) or Het-Heru (Hathor).

Regardless of the name, humans saw the personality of a motherly woman within the waterways, the rain, and the harvest. There are metaphorical correlations that may explain this concept. Of course, a people would see their primary source of sustenance as a mother of sorts—feeding and nurturing their people. If you lived near the ocean, it would represent this principle. If you lived by a river, it might take on these qualities. It is also understandable that a people would see the fluctuating activity of these bodies of water as the temperaments and actions of a conscious living woman, full of personality and power. Similarly, the Bushongo of the Congo believed in a god of plants named Chonganda, to whom they would appeal for blessings from the plant kingdom.

All over the continent, this sort of logic existed. For this reason, you can still find practitioners across the continent of Africa and beyond going to nature for their needs and desires, both spiritual and worldly.[14] Their belief that divine intelligence and personality are

---

14 John Oluwasegun Ojo, *Understanding West African Traditional Religion* (Popoola Printers, 1999), 63.

present in the plants, animals, and elements is fundamentally aligned with the idea of spiritual gardening. In order to access this wisdom and bring it into your hobby, it helps to be open to the concepts of communication and unity with your plants. This isn't to say that one must worship one's garden, but it lends credibility to the idea of consciousness being present within the process of a garden.

If we look to the Norse people of northern Europe, we will see more examples of connectivity between the spirit world and the natural physical manifestation. In their cosmology, the entire universe, called the Nine Realms, is said to be held together and supported by a divine tree. They called this tree Yggdrasill, and it held great significance in all aspects of their belief system.[15] Seeing it as the support and foundation of all life throughout the universe, Norse people often decorated and held ceremonies around a large, old tree to symbolize this great divine Tree of Life. This also affected the planning of their homes and villages, which were often plotted around this sort of ceremonial tree in order to mimic their vision of the cosmos.[16]

Aside from this, they subscribed to other spiritualized concepts of their environment and understood that the divine forces of the world move through nature and her elements to affect humanity. Deities such as Sif, goddess of harvest and land, Njord, god of the sea and wind, and the beloved Thor, god of thunder and storms, all exemplify the Norse reverence for nature. What caused this civilization to see the world in this way? What benefit, if any, did it have on their way of life?

We can also look to the Celtic cultures of western Europe for this kind of philosophy. The ancient peoples of what are now Germany, France, England, Ireland, and Scotland shared a common culture

---

15 John Lindow, *Norse Mythology: A Guide to the Gods, Heroes, Rituals, and Beliefs* (London: Oxford University Press, 2002).
16 Rudolf Simek, *Dictionary of Northern Mythology*, trans. Angela Hall (Woodbridge, UK, and Rochester, NY: Boydell and Brewer, 1993), 375–376.

that can be called Celtic. Having also held trees and certain herbs in high esteem, the Celts are thought to have practiced their own form of nature religion. Like the cultures of Africa and Asia, and others in northern Europe, Celts saw consciousness, or spirits, in all of nature. This was thought to be not an organized religion per se, but one of several small local practices with common perceptions about reality.[17]

It is also commonly believed that these Celtic societies venerated some of the same nature deities. For instance, the goddess Dana, or Anu, was considered the mother deity of the land, or the earth element, for the common culture. Similarly, Boyne was thought to be the goddess of the great rivers of Ireland—specifically, the one that still bears her name. Then there is the horned Green Man, who is thought to be the god of the wild, plants, and all greenery on Earth. Some version of him existed in the beliefs of the ancient people of Wales, Scotland, and Ireland. The common theme is that the natural world shows personality traits, awareness, and consciousness that can be communicated with.

One striking similarity between disparate beliefs is the idea of a Tree of Life. This conception of a world tree, known in Irish Gaelic as Crann Bethadh, is almost identical to those found in other parts of the world. It follows the idea that this tree connects all life on Earth and serves as an attachment between our world and the spiritual dimensions of reality. The ancient Celts are said to have honored this tree in the design of their villages and homes by allowing the oldest, largest tree to remain alive when clearing their targeted property.

It is interesting to note that the work of modern botanists, specifically Suzanne Simard, supports the ecological benefits of this practice. Through reforestation efforts and research, it has been scientifically proven that repopulating an old-growth forest

---

17 Barry Cunliffe, *The Ancient Celts* (Oxford and New York: Oxford University Press, 1997).

clearing can be done most effectively in cases where the oldest trees are allowed to remain standing.[18]

Were the Celts onto something in doing this centuries ago? Were they instructed to do this through reverence and communion with nature? The Celtic Tree of Life is still revered in Western society as a symbol of the importance of nature and our relationship to it. This symbol can be found on all kinds of jewelry and clothing even in the present day, a testament to ancient peoples' understanding of the natural world.

Last but certainly not least, let's look to Native American culture. The American Indians encompassed many peoples and cultures and belief systems. However, several wonderful commonalities exist. Native American spirituality almost always consists of reliance on the understanding of the elements, belief in the presence of consciousness in all the natural world, a microcosmic-macrocosmic relationship with the cosmos, use of plants for medicine, and connection with the spiritual.[19] Though there are differences in their stories and personalities, all the deities that can be found in the indigenous beliefs of America are embodied in the natural environment.

One such deity with particular significance to agriculture is the Corn Mother. As corn has always been an important mainstay crop to natives all over North and Central America, they developed multiple versions of this goddess, varying from tribe to tribe. The importance of this crop and its nurturing presence became archetypal to the peoples of this part of the world. The Cherokee called her Selu, whereas the Aztec version was Chicomecoatl. In some cases, this spiritual energy was assigned to multiple personalities known as the Corn Maidens. In either case, native people personi-

---

18 Jason S. Barker et al., "Ectomycorrhizal Fungal Community Assembly on Regenerating Douglas-Fir After Wildfire and Clearcut Harvesting," *Oecologia* 172 (2013): 1179–1189.

19 David M. Jones and Brian L. Molyneaux, *Mythology of the American Nations: An Illustrated Encyclopedia of the Gods, Heroes, Spirits, Sacred Places, Rituals, and Ancient Beliefs of the North American Indian, Inuit, Aztec, Inca, and Maya Nations* (London: Hermes House, 2004).

fied and deified corn as a way of explaining its importance and use in their cultures. Like the Greeks, they used mythology to explain the properties of not only corn but also all the different plants and medicinal herbs of the land.

The legend of Sage among the Hasinai Indians of what is now Texas is the story of a young native maiden who falls in love with a star. She becomes so smitten with the star that she wants to die in order to be with him. The young maiden goes to an old medicine woman and asks how she can die properly to join her beloved. The old woman wants to help her but doesn't believe that life should be disregarded so frivolously, so she comes up with a plan for the girl. The old woman turns the girl into a plant, and the star comes down to her and turns into a white dust that powders the girl's leaves. The star turns into the flowers of the plant, and the sage plant, as we know it, is born from this union.[20]

This well-known medicinal plant has had great significance not only for native peoples but also for any that understand the power of herbalism. To this day, sage is used for a range of ailments such as respiratory diseases, infertility, and cognitive disorders. It is also a skin anesthetic and a diuretic. The creation of these kinds of stories around an herb like sage illustrates the significance it held in the culture. These mythological explanations for the natural world and the elements, and their properties, were present in the indigenous cultures of America, just as they were in other parts of the world. By now, one should see a common thread that runs throughout humanity's cultures—a philosophy that acknowledges and respects the consciousness within nature and seeks to commune with it for self-realization and health.

Surely, there is a reason cultures separated by distance and time took a similar view of nature. Could there be validity to this way of seeing the world? Is this a natural perspective for humans

---

20 Florence Stratton, *When the Storm God Rides: Tejas and Other Indian Legends* (New York: Scribner's, 1936), 109–113.

when given enough time in contact with the environment? Are there advantages to working with nature and respecting her as a divine force, rather than seeking conquest? Is it possible that the value wasn't so much in what these civilizations believed, but rather in how this belief shaped their relationship to the planet?

Some would attribute this to evolutionary development of culture and society, as if these groups and their ancient ways were primitive. However, even today, the veneration of nature in some shape or form still exists. As a gardener, it is useful for you to acknowledge these connections because, if nothing else, they are the foundation of our agricultural understanding. It was those who saw spiritual depth and power in nature that bothered to study it, be with it, and understand its ways. It was the people who loved and adored the various forms of plant life who learned their secrets.

Like them, you can come to know and embody this wisdom. The amazing gift of gardening is that it gives you a personalized, controlled way to experience these truths. It will become clear that a holistic understanding of your hobby can open you up to a more spiritual connection with your garden and, therefore, the natural world. Just accepting the possibility of having a deeper connection to your plants is a step in the direction toward expanding your consciousness. How much more fulfilling might it be to have intuitive understanding of your plants and the needs of the growing process? How awesome would you feel about the ability to pick and effectively use medicine grown from your own hand? Wouldn't you enjoy knowing that your own love and attention can be sown, grown, and returned through your diet in a real way?

There is consciousness present in the plant kingdom, as well as wisdom and divine energy. Through this consciousness, we can not only be guided in our own affairs and health, but we may also learn a thing or two about what it means to be in harmony with the Earth itself. It is not necessary to seek religious significance in the garden. Rather, if one just remains open-minded and respectful of the process, the greater significance of the garden will reveal itself in time. The point of this exploration is to expose one's spirit, and source information and nourishment from the garden that will bring balance and peace into your life. We can accomplish this by marrying the holistic practices of Ayurveda and Yoga with your enjoyment of gardening. The meditative exercises and dietary wisdom of Vedic culture will allow you to realize a special kind of unity and synchronicity with nature. These and similar wisdom traditions can be sourced for inspiration and understanding that, when applied to gardening, will bear great fruit.

However, the depth of this relationship will be totally dependent on your own willingness to experience it. Sure, you may not perceive divinity within your garden in the same way our ancestors did, but you may come to understand how they were capable of such perceptions. Like them, we can come to see the consciousness and unity in our natural world. We can develop a relationship to it. In this way, our garden can become more than just a place where herbs and vegetables grow.

CHAPTER 2

PLANT GURUS

"We abuse land because we regard it as a
commodity belonging to us. When we see land as
a community to which we belong, we may begin
to use it with love and respect."

—*Aldo Leopold*

Let's now return to the subject of consciousness. What is consciousness? Is it merely the ability to think? Does it require a brain? Are there different levels or kinds of consciousness? Does our place at the top of the food chain automatically signify that humans are the highest form of consciousness on the planet? What standards of measurement could be used for such an assessment?

The collective human understanding of consciousness has been problematic in our relationship with the planet and our fellow beings. Since we barely understand who we are as consciousness, humans tend to overlook or disregard the right to life of other beings on this planet. We are getting better and more aware of our environment, but there is still much work to be done. As we grow in consciousness, humanity may become more respectful and understanding of the other forms of consciousness present in the plants, animals, and processes around us.

Much of what we know about consciousness has just led to more confusion. One of the fundamental hurdles of any concrete study of it is known as the hard problem of consciousness, which states that no matter how much we learn about the observable biological processes of the human being, we cannot explain why these processes are accompanied by or produce experience. However, we have been able to use science and technology to make amazing observations about consciousness. We now know so much about the mind and how it works from an objective standpoint.

It is the first-person experiential qualities of consciousness that cause problems for the scientific model, however. As philosopher David Chalmers once wrote in *The Conscious Mind: In Search of a Fundamental Theory*, "Materialism is a beautiful and compelling view of the world, but to account for consciousness, we have to go beyond the resources it provides."[21] Despite our best efforts in medical science and psychology, we still haven't answered some basic questions about consciousness. For example, what is it, exactly? Why do we experience qualia (observing properties of things as distinct from objects with those properties) or have subjective experience at all? Our scientific community can explain the mechanics of sight in detail, but it fails miserably at explaining why we see, or what it is in this mind-body being that sees. As Chalmers goes on to state, "We know consciousness far more intimately than we know the rest of the world, but we understand the rest of the world far better than we understand consciousness."[22]

Even though the wisdom traditions of the world have taught us the way to self-discovery, we try to understand consciousness by methods of science, overlooking the important role our own consciousness plays in the process. That isn't exactly working. It falls victim to an age-old conundrum, which is that consciousness cannot perceive itself. Perception, itself, is getting in the way of perceiving: A knife

---

21 David Chalmers, *The Conscious Mind: In Search of a Fundamental Theory* (New York: Oxford University Press, 1996), 95–106.
22 Ibid.

cannot cut itself, so they say. In other words, to understand consciousness one must not use the logical, thinking mind.

That isn't to say that we'll never understand it, but as of now, consciousness continues to remain a mystery. How arrogant is it, then, for humans to assume that we know everything about it and can place limits on other forms of consciousness, while barely understanding our own? If our ancestors acknowledged and revered the spirits of the plant kingdom, what was it that registered with them? How were they able to perceive and respect consciousness in plants? And why? Maybe there was some reason, or some benefit to this perception.

What we *can* determine with some accuracy is intelligence, although this too is a term that is a source of debate within the field of psychology. Generally, intelligence can be understood as the ability to make decisions. According to Merriam-Webster's online dictionary, the latest definitions for *intelligence* are as follows:

(1): the ability to learn or understand or to deal with new or trying situations: the skilled use of reason
(2): the ability to apply knowledge to manipulate one's enviroment or to think abstractly as measured by objective criteria.[23]

Alfred Binet, the revered French psychologist and the inventor of the IQ test, once explained intelligence another way, saying, "*Comprehension, inventiveness, direction,* and *criticism*: Intelligence is contained in these four words."[24] And it is that comprehension and inventiveness that marks intelligence no matter where one finds it.

For our purposes, we can stick with these two definitions, as others refer to information and are distinctly human in nature. The point of analyzing this definition is to determine whether we have such a monopoly on intelligence, as we seem to think. Also, are the intelligences of other beings in line with our current understanding?

---

23 "Intelligence," Merriam-Webster, https://www.merriam-webster.com.
24 Alfred Binet, *Modern Ideas About Children*, trans. Suzanne Heisler (Suzanne Heisler, 1975).

If we can arrive at a more expansive understanding of intelligence, possibly, we could understand how the shamans can believe that the herbs tell them what medicines to choose, or how a people might see their divine mother figure within the harvest of their crops. Maybe there is more consciousness around us than we are aware of. If your plants have some form of sentience, wouldn't it be beneficial to garden in harmony with them? By and large, the scientific community has focused on finding some form of nervous system as the necessary requirement for consciousness. However, our mystics and sages have long told us that there is consciousness in everything.

Is it possible for a plant, a single-celled organism, or a crystal to have consciousness? If these do, then what does that mean for the brain? Can consciousness exist without a brain? If so, in what forms?

Let's look at the first definition and determine whether it applies to plant life. When defined as "the ability to learn or understand or to deal with new or trying situations," one can say that intelligence is present in plant life. As Stefano Mancuso, plant neurobiologist and author of *Brilliant Green: The Surprising History and Science of Plant Intelligence*, once said, "Intelligence is the ability to solve problems, and plants are amazingly good in solving their problems."[25]

As we see from several animal species, like jellyfish, sea anemones, and earthworms, a brain is not always necessary for life, and even if it is present, it can look vastly different across species. Researchers such as Rainer Hedrich and his team in Würzburg, Germany, have suggested that the phloem of plants acts as a sort of nervous system, conducting electricity and information similar to our own. Phloem is the vascular tissue of plants, usually thought to transport nutrients from the leaves to the rest of the plant. But Hedrich's research showed that there is much more going on. He writes, "In plants, the phloem can be considered as a 'green cable' that allows the transmission of action potentials (APs) induced by

---

25 Jeremy Hance, "Are Plants Intelligent? New Book Says Yes," *Guardian*, August 4, 2015.

stimuli such as wounding and cold."[26] This bioelectric conductivity found in phloem, along with the roots, could prove to be the plant version of a nervous system. Further research is needed to find out more about the "neural networks" of plants.

Regardless of the presence of a brain, there are some fantastically organized and adaptable plants out there. To say they are intelligent may be arguable, but it is undeniable that an intelligence of some sort has produced these marvels. Is it possible that our limited understanding of consciousness has placed barriers in our perception of the other beings of this planet? If so, what can be gained from reversing this view and treating plants as sentient beings? To gardeners, it's pretty obvious that happy plants will make better produce. Why not invest attention toward the possibility of cooperation with your garden and the life within it? The process of taking this humane, spiritually aware approach will yield its own fruits and infuse depth into your gardening hobby simply by encouraging you to understand the life of your plants in new contexts.

The highly adaptive nature of plant life is a primary sign that they can perceive and react to their environment, albeit in ways that we may not fully understand. One of the best examples of this is a process that humans also participate in: pollination. Most people probably don't consider our role in this process, but humans and other creatures are moving plant material around all the time. We eat their fruit and disperse their seeds, we carry their spurs and spores in our travels throughout the land, and we selectively harvest and cultivate them, directly impacting the future of their species. As a result, these immobile creatures can propagate in lands far away.

Surely, as living but stationary creatures, plants have had to come up with some creative means to reproduce. How would this be possible without consciousness? There are many common examples of this kind of reproductive ingenuity, from dandelion seeds lifted on the wind to helicopter-like maple tree seeds to spurring plants, and, of

---

26 Rainer Hedrich et al. "Electrical Wiring and Long-Distance Plant Communication," *Trends in Plant Science* 21, no. 5 (May 2016): 376–387.

course, those that produce fruits and vegetables. In nature's timeless wisdom, plants adapted to create delicious, nutrient-rich produce as a ruse to get mobile creatures to eat their seeds and spread them across the Earth. To deny that this behavior is "the ability to learn or understand or to deal with new or trying situations" is missing the point. The main reason that flowers are so eye-catching and aromatic is to attract the attention of various creatures in the environment that can help them propagate. Similar to fruits, flowers help plants pull in co-conspirators to accomplish their reproductive goals.

It is even more profound to think that these plants are medicinal and have other benefits that causally relate to human consciousness. This is indicative of an extremely long symbiosis between humanity and the plant world. Is this by accident? Could they have adapted their properties in order to increase their value to humans? It is unknown how such a process of adaptation would be initiated, but certainly, many plant species have benefited from human consumption and use. If you consider the common herbs we use, how many of them would be scarce on the planet if it were left entirely up to nature? How many tomatoes, potatoes, or roses would there be if they were growing wild?

Human cultivation and use have favored certain plants, guaranteeing the security of their species. Since reproductive success is such a huge investment of energy, maybe plants have somehow decided to work smarter, not harder. Who is to say that the plants themselves did not participate? By providing humanity with the nourishment, medicine, and sensual pleasure we need, certain plants have been winning. This has come at the expense of others, but, to the point, there are biological advantages.

Consider this: You and a bee see on two totally different color and light spectrums and have distinctly different olfactory systems,

yet you both see and smell a beautiful flower and are drawn to it. The bee may take pollen, while you may get medicine, but you both come to this immobile plant, and, as a result, it is getting its goals accomplished—giving and receiving in harmony with the world around it. The whole spectacle is miraculous and deeply spiritual when seen in this way.

Many notable adaptations indicate that plants have a sort of consciousness within that is interacting with the surrounding environment for its survival. Take carnivorous plants such as Venus flytraps, pitcher plants, and sundews, which trap prey with specialized leaves and digest them with fluids. These plants are presumed to have adapted this way due to growing in areas where either sun, soil, or water quality is such that nutrients are required in another form. This adaptation is a sign of consciousness. In some ways, you could say any adaptation is a sign of consciousness, exhibiting change caused by a perception or registering of stimuli. Nonetheless, this is an example of a simple lower level of consciousness. Even at a most basic level, we must wonder what it is that "thinks" to change? And if this consciousness reacts to stimuli in its environment, what are its reactions to you? How does a plant adapt to your behaviors and energy? Can your actions be more conducive to the growth and health of your garden?

Another strong but lesser-known example of adaptation is the pyrophytic plants—those found in regions that routinely experience fire damage. They have adapted some ingenious measures. For instance, lodgepole pines and eucalyptus seal their seeds in specialized resins that are activated and released only once touched by the heat of fire. Likewise, members of the fire lily genus will flower in order to welcome pollinators only after a scorching. Some, like the majestic stone pines and ponderosa pines, simply developed their crowns much higher in order to avoid treetops being consumed by forest fires.[27]

---

27 Melissa Petruzzello, "Playing with Wildfire: 5 Amazing Adaptations of Pyrophytic Plants," Britannica, https://www.britannica.com/list/5-amazing-adaptations-of-pyrophytic-plants.

These plant behaviors clearly indicate the reaction of some form of consciousness to its environment—if not an individual consciousness, then a collective awareness that alters behavior and activity based on these outside factors. If one were inclined to close observation of plants, one would see a world of actions and reactions, adjustments, movements, partnerships, exchange, relationships, life, and death. Is it possible that there is a reason our ancestors saw personality and drama within nature? What can we learn from paying more attention to these actions? Is there a reason so many of these observations became attached, either directly or through metaphor, to stories of spiritual significance?

Take Borneo's pitcher plant, which has evolved a variety of adaptations to attract and benefit the local bat population in exchange for its nitrogen-rich feces. By forming leaves that provide ideal and preferred roosts for these bats, *Nepenthes hemsleyana* can get one of the most valuable resources of nutrition available in its environment. The plant's shape and reflective surface essentially "call" to bats via the animal's echolocation ability, summoning them to find rest there. As the bats defecate, making themselves feel right at home, the plant's pitcher leaves collect and process the guano into the food that the plant needs.[28]

Some varieties of this species are probably holding even more secrets indicative of conscious adaptation, as there are those with "fangs" (*Nepenthes bicalcarata*) and other adaptations that have similar effects on other creatures like ants and rodents. While this may be an exotic, tropical plant, it shows the marvels that plants are capable of. These fantastic-looking plants didn't just end up with these highly creative means by way of blind materialistic automation. This was an amazingly effective adaptation to a dire situation. How would these plants know to create these kinds of petals unless there was some kind of observation of bat activity? This is a true example of a harmonious, symbiotic, mutually beneficial relation

---

[28] Stephanie Pappas, "How Hungry Pitcher Plants Get the Poop They Need," Live Science, July 9, 2015

ship. Plants are accomplishing feats like this all the time right under our noses. Maybe there is something that we can learn from these simple yet incredible displays of wisdom and harmony.

Also, consider that your plants are reacting to more than just how much water and sun they get. As a gardener, you are a routine, if not daily, source of stimulus and interaction for the plants you are growing. What adaptations might your plants be taking to your presence and energy? How can you use this to your advantage as a grower and human being?

Let's look at the species *Arabidopsis thaliana*, absolutely amazing and vital to the study of plant consciousness and reactivity. The common mustard plant, growing along roadsides and in pastures and wildlands, is generally thought of as a weed. However, it was the first plant to have its genome sequenced, which has opened the doors to our understanding of just how conscious plants really are. The most interesting feature of this plant is its scientifically verifiable reaction to sound. Research has shown that playing the sound of an insect chewing in the vicinity of a mustard plant causes it to release chemicals and hormones that give it immunity and deter insects.[29] Essentially, exposed to a hostile stimulus, it defends itself!

These experiments were conducted purely with sound played electronically. How do these plants hear anything, let alone the quiet chews of a caterpillar? What within the plant registers the sound? And, even more intriguing, what decides to produce the chemical? What decides that this sound is deleterious to its well-being. Through technology, we can witness a plant "hearing" something and reacting to it. This is monumental to our understanding of plants as actual beings possessing a sense of self and of environmental awareness. Imagine the layers of consciousness that truly reside beyond our growing, yet limited, understanding of them. When one decides to cultivate plants, whether in a garden or indoors, one is taking on more than pieces of nature's furniture. These are not lifeless objects, and to some degree, they are aware. Treating them as such can only be beneficial to their growth.

---

29 H. M. Appel and R. B. Cocroft, "Plants Respond to Leaf Vibrations Caused by Insect Herbivore Chewing," *Oecologia* 175 (2014): 1257–1266.

The amazing thing about building this kind of relationship with your plants is the subtle yet profound effects it can have on your life. The time you spend mindfully caring for your garden can be transformed into breaks in your routine for reflection and silence. These peaceful moments of unity and nurturing can be meditative. Then there are the many benefits of getting choice produce from a happy, lively plant. A spiritual gardening practice connects us to the process in a way that is harmonious both in energy and execution. The foundation of such a transformative hobby is inherently rooted in respecting the life and well-being of the plants. No matter what level of consciousness you perceive in them, you can benefit from acknowledging it only if you plan to cultivate them.

We learn a lot about beneficial relationships with plants from the insect kingdom. Take, for example, the findings from the work of entomologist Jennifer Thaler from the University of California, Davis. In a 1999 study, Thaler and her team found that tomato plants could form alliances with cooperative insects for mutual benefits. The tomato has built a remarkably interesting defense tactic against the beet armyworm. When an armyworm feeds on the tomato's leaves, the plant releases a chemical compound known as jasmonic acid that attracts a tiny parasitic wasp to the scene of the crime. These wasps parasitize the beet armyworm caterpillars, thus saving the day for the tomato. As Thaler said, "The plants are essentially sending up a chemical smoke signal to attract the wasps." The wasps get the benefit of planting their eggs in new juicy hosts, where the young will hatch and feed, while the tomato gets a welcomed defender. Examples like this indicate an awareness.[30]

The debate within the scientific community over whether these behaviors denote consciousness is ongoing and greatly polarized. However, both sides would probably agree that there are benefits to understanding more about how these kinds of mechanisms work

---

[30] "Caterpillars Foiled When Tomato Plants Summon Parasitic Wasps," ScienceDaily, June 22, 1999, https://www.sciencedaily.com/releases/1999/06/990622055654.htm.

and how these relationships come to be established in nature. This understanding can lead to safer forms of pesticide, the discovery of natural ways of optimizing growth, and creating harmonious gardening techniques that are effective and gentle on the environment.

You may also find it interesting to know that plants communicate with each other, which should uproot any doubts about the presence of plant consciousness. Surely, something that actively communicates with another is conscious in every sense of the word. Awareness, reaction, and desire to communicate are all displayed within this one act. This is not to mention that the plant is doing this while its body conducts numerous other vital functions for its survival, similar to the way you are able to read these words while creating new blood cells and breathing. No mechanical system simply does this. It is the presence of consciousness that is capable of such actions.

The average person does not see a plant as another living being. If considered at all, plants are an effect of nature, a characteristic of the environment, not as beings sharing the environment and living out their own life purposes. But research as far back as 1997 suggests that plants not only send and receive signals but also respond, therefore having dialogue right below our feet through what is sometimes referred to as the fungal internet.

One notable contributor to this understanding is Suzanne Simard, a professor of forest ecology at the University of British Columbia in Vancouver whose work was briefly mentioned above. Her phenomenal work in this field has opened many doors to our understanding and exploration of how plants communicate. Simard discovered that Douglas fir and paper birch trees communicate with each other through a network of fungal mycelia living between their root systems.

As this is a common feature of the root systems of forests, her discovery gave rise to unlocking an entire network underneath the ground—of cooperation and communication between plant species.[31]

---

31 Suzanne Simard et al., "Resource Transfer Between Plants Through Ectomycorrhizal Networks," in *Mycorrhizal Networks*, edited by T. R. Horton (Berlin: Springer, 2015).

Fungi all over the natural world typically have a mutually beneficial symbiosis with the plant life around them. These fungi have spread their own kind of root system, attaching their mycelia to the host's roots. These mycelia can connect with other fungi over long distances and help their host by providing extra nutrients and water retention from the soil in exchange for carbohydrates.

The key here is that these fungi end up creating a highly conductive bioelectrical and chemical network for their hosts to communicate through. The existence of mycorrhiza, or fungi growing in symbiosis with trees, is not a new discovery. However, they have been given renewed interest due to the work of people like Simard, who have researched this feature of sharing information. Their study of this phenomenon has raised awareness in the scientific community of just how cooperative and communicative the plant life of the forest really is. The mycelia of the fungi kingdom provide a natural kind of internet, by which the plants "speak" to one another, as well as provide mutual assistance in defense and growth. This discovery is astounding, and there is still much to learn.[32]

In a series of experiments by Simard and her team, they deduced that trees conduct two-way conversations all the time concerning conditions in the environment, including diseases and predatory insects. One of the most fascinating discoveries has been that they also can sense ill health or lack in others and produce nutrients and chemicals to help one another grow and sustain. Furthermore, trees can sense their kin and show affinity toward them. Surely, with more research into these topics, humanity will find even more complexity.

The takeaway from this is to note the heightened sense of connection and awareness plants have within their environment. It's as if nature gifted plants with an amazing ability to tap into the environment as a compensation for a mostly stationary life. They can use everything around them for some benefit while still being in harmony with it all. Could there be a human equivalent to this ability? Is there

---

32 Sabine C. Jung et al., "Mycorrhiza-Induced Resistance and Priming of Plant Defenses," *Journal of Chemical Ecology* 38 (2012), 651–664.

some version of this kind of harmony that humans can experience? What other wisdom can we possibly learn from plant observation? If plants have developed ways of communicating among themselves and the other members of the natural world, is it possible that they receive signals from us?

Even in the common plants of our gardens, there are expressions of consciousness that we can learn from. Researchers at South China Agricultural University in Guangzhou have found similar communication capabilities via the mycelia of the root system of tomato plants. They exposed tomatoes to harmful fungi and found that other nearby tomatoes also put up defenses, as though under attack. Scientist Ren Sen Zeng reported on this study, saying, "We suggest that tomato plants can 'eavesdrop' on defense responses and increase their disease resistance against potential pathogens."[33] This means that even a common tomato has awareness of self as well as of other tomatoes, and of environmental threats, including disease, weather conditions, and hostile forms of life. Even more fascinating is that we are just beginning to understand how it is also capable of communicating these experiences and information to others.

In studies conducted at the Swedish University of Agricultural Sciences in Uppsala, ecologists found that plants help each other grow, identify and recognize one another, and even alert each other about danger. Lead scientist Velemir Ninkovic and his team have shown many complexities in the root systems of plants and their use outside of merely soaking up soil nutrients. In one study, they gently stroked the leaves of one *Zea mays*, or corn plant, while ignoring adjacent plants.

It has long been known that touch can stimulate growth in plants, so the point of this experiment was to see whether these benefits were transferred from one plant to the other. They found that the untouched neighboring corn plants also experienced significant growth and vitality through their actions. Essentially, the touched plants registered this stimulus and conferred the benefits of their

---

33 Yuan Yuan Song et al., "Interplant Communication of Tomato Plants Through Underground Common Mycorrhizal Networks," *PloS ONE* 5, no. 10 (2010): e13324.

experience with others. Ninkovic states, "Our results show that the aboveground plant-plant communication by brief touch can provoke responses in nearby nontouched plants through belowground communication. It thus suggests that plant-plant belowground communication is modified by aboveground mechanical stimulation."[34]

This means that plants not only sense their environment in multiple ways but also speak to each other concerning their environment across distances that we may have never considered. This kind of community-building behavior, of shared resources and mutually beneficial transactions, is much needed in our human society today. Consider that a little more time spent connecting to this kind of energy and essentially working with it through your garden can open the pathways to more of these behaviors in your own life. Notice how certain herbs, like oregano and basil, have similar likes and therefore grow well together, complementing each other's insect-fighting abilities and naturally respecting growing space without crowding— thriving in harmony, sharing, and growing.

Can we not do the same with our fellow humans? The beauty of gardening with spiritual awareness is that you become more in tune with this kind of subtle wisdom and guidance. You notice the world of activity happening within the silent spaces of your time in the garden. You see the small but significant growth and change in your plants and understand their meanings. You cultivate an understanding of how the activity of the plants is connected to you and the nourishment that you can gain from them. By respecting plants as living beings with awareness, gardeners open themselves up to learn more from working with plants than just how to grow them better. They can grow to see themselves and what they may need to grow as well.

If you still find yourself in doubt as to whether plants are conscious, you may find it interesting to know that they are also capable of learning.

---

34 Ali Elhakeem et al., "Aboveground Mechanical Stimuli Affect Belowground Plant-Plant Communication," *PLoS ONE* 13, no. 5 (2018): e0195646.

Learning is a very distinct characteristic of sentience, indicating not only intelligence but also memory. When a being can remember an experience and choose to react differently when confronted with similar circumstances again, this is also a kind of wisdom being exhibited.

Work done by Australian researcher Monica Gagliano has shed light on just how adaptive plants can be in this way.[35] She has written several books on her research and experiences of plant gnosophysiology, or cognition. In one of her experiments, Gagliano was able to show that mimosa plants could learn through a Pavlovian method of exposing them to routine drops of water and analyzing their reactions. The mimosa plant, *Mimosa pudica*, is a fascinating member of the plant kingdom that moves quickly enough for humans to observe. When its specialized leaves are touched, they close to protect themselves from harm, reopening after a few minutes in the absence of apparent danger. The plant's reactive nature makes it a perfect subject for understanding plant consciousness.

In Gagliano's results, the plants reacted ordinarily at first, but after receiving several drops of water over a period of time, they learned that there was no danger and stopped reacting. This learned reaction was observed up to several weeks afterward, suggesting that the plant had, in fact, identified and remembered the experimental experience. This could be verified even after the plants were returned to a more natural benign setting, showing that the plant itself remembered this and was not merely reacting to environmental cues. In a paper for online publication, Gagliano said, "This relatively long-lasting learned behavioral change as a result of previous experience matches the persistence of habituation effects observed in many animals." Later in the paper, she also states that "plants may lack brains and neural tissues, but they do possess a sophisticated calcium-based signaling network in their cells similar to animals' memory processes."[36]

---

35 Monica Gagliano et al., "Experience Teaches Plants to Learn Faster and Forget Slower in Environments Where It Matters," *Oecologia* 175 (2014): 63–72.
36 Ibid.

You may not see the relevance of this right away, but let's extract some wisdom from the mimosa experiment. How many times in your life have you met the same stimuli, whether it be a person, a thought, an emotion, a relationship, or a behavior, with the same response? Do you react, or have you ever been reactive, in this way, sensing danger or creating problems for yourself where there aren't any? Like the mimosa, you can learn to relax, recognize the fear or reflex for what it is, and change your behavior. You, too, can learn to soften your stance against the dangerous world outside. If you observe the behaviors of the plants in your garden, you may glean this kind of simple wisdom from what you see. You can see correlation between their activity and your own experiences.

Gagliano's study of plant consciousness has also yielded significant evidence that plants can "hear" the sound of rushing water and grow toward it. An additional field of research for Gagliano is the ability of plants to produce sound. Others have picked up this new research, and it will be exciting to see what is uncovered about the communication capabilities of the plant world. She and a few like-minded researchers have introduced the concept of plant cognitive ecology to the scientific community, despite ridicule from peers and colleagues. Their dedication to both science and understanding consciousness have laid the groundwork for this topic to be explored by even the biggest skeptics, providing verifiable science to back up these claims that many mystics have known of since the beginning of time.

As we cultivate our understanding of nature's intelligence, we have to wonder whether it is possible to have direct connection and communication with the plant kingdom. After all, we are also a part of this planetary consciousness and its activity. No matter how out of balance we may seem at times, we are still part of the community of organisms living on this planet. If plants can communicate with each other and share mutually beneficial relationships with the animal and fungal kingdoms, where do we come into the picture? Are humans solely a destructive force in this world, an outsider? Or are we simply not getting the signal?

There are those throughout history who have developed very peculiar relationships with plants, which inspires us to explore the possibilities. However, much is left to learn. It's possible that there is a reason plants are reported to grow better when sung to, or why the spiritually inclined like to go into nature to speak to the divine. If it were possible that your garden could "hear" you, what sounds would be best suited for your mutual health? What words or vibrations could you produce to optimize the vitality of your garden?

To some, there is no doubt that communication is possible with plants. In fact, a study conducted by the United Kingdom's Royal Horticultural Society showed evidence suggesting that not only do plants "hear" us and react to our vibrations and tones, they also have preferences. This experiment showed a significant affinity for female human voices over males in tomato plants. There was no clear-cut reason for this preference, but its implications are aligned with what has been said throughout this entire chapter: Plants are not mindless objects of the environment, but conscious living beings that affect and are affected by those around them.

This notion of plant consciousness and communication is at the heart of the philosophy of the Findhorn Foundation in Scotland. The members of this community of spiritual seekers and metaphysical enthusiasts have long held that their leadership has been in communication with the plant kingdom. They teach methods of plant communication and the belief that anyone with an open mind can receive these intuitive messages.

While the Findhorn community is regarded as a New Age, spiritual utopian society, what sets it apart from others is that the organization has demonstrated results of this communication. In the 1960s, founding members Eileen Caddy, Peter Caddy, and Dorothy Maclean used their own spiritual communication methods to contact what they called the nature spirits of the land. In doing so, they were given guidance in several aspects of human endeavor, including the care of and relationship with the plant kingdom. Using the information they were given, this group was able to produce exceptionally large, healthy produce and soon gained many followers.

The teachings of these nature spirits, as given to the founders, is still followed to this day by a community of thousands worldwide. While some observers may remain skeptical about these ideas, many of the group's experiences and findings do suggest that there is something to their methods. Some of the communications from the natural world merely serve as formal introductions between these spirits and humanity, while some carry a very distinct message. For example, the spirit of the South American yerba mate tree is reported to have said, "You drink of us, and we are integrated into your bodies. We would rather integrate into your hearts and spirits that you might see us as your sisters/brothers, as your kin. This is the truth of it, for all life is kin to all other life. We know this and would have you know this too."[37]

This and many other messages were outlined by Judy McAllister, a member of the Findhorn community, in her book *Forest Voices: When Nature Speaks.* Whether one lends credence to this kind of experience or not, it has proven helpful and wise for many people all over the world. It cannot be disregarded as woo-woo, New Age talk when the proof is literally in the produce. Findhorn members ascribe to an ideal that promotes working with the more subtle influences of nature and tapping into one's own spiritual capabilities.

In *Forest Voices*, McAllister gives some easy-to-follow advice on how to establish communication with plants in your own life. Even though we are focusing on spiritual connection through gardening, some of these methods are synergistic with what you will find in this book. Tips like showing appreciation and gratitude toward plants, spending time with them, opening intuition to receive their communications, and detailed interest in their development r ing true whether one is in the forest or the garden. The teachings of the Findhorn community have value in that they encourage us all to be better citizens of this planet and they promote reverence

---

37 Thomas Miller, "Listening to the Voices of Trees," Findhorn Foundation, December 13, 2018, https://www.findhorn.org/blog/tree-voices.

for the plant beings of the world. Although this is not scientific verification of plant consciousness, the results of communicating with plants are undeniable to those who follow and share these teachings.

After all is said and done, what can we deduce? It should be clear that plants have their own kind of conscious awareness and intelligence. This enables them to adapt and manipulate their environment according to their needs. It should also be apparent that plants communicate with each other and other forms of life. This field of study deserves much more attention and will continue to grow as more of modern society embraces the plant world. We can only imagine at this point what will be in store for human-plant relations moving forward, but there is encouragement in the fact that more people are realizing that there may be something to this idea of plant consciousness.

The important takeaway from this is that plants are living beings too, capable of their own form of amazing feats and adaptation. We have looked at several examples in this chapter, and the entire planet can provide opportunities to experience this in your own life. For the purposes of this book, you are encouraged to simply sit with this information and keep an open mind. We will explore some personalized methods of achieving this awareness of the plants around you and the best ways to treat them for balance and harmony.

As you are reading this, you may not live in or have access to wild, untamed nature like some. You may be interested in experiencing more intimate contact with the plant kingdom yet live in an environment that doesn't seem conducive to this kind of relationship. However, the practice of gardening can help place you in direct connection with nature and the realization of oneness. Although a well-cultivated garden is a controlled environment, it can be just as informative and rich, with the opportunity to experience a relationship with plants. In doing so, we can reap benefits of stress relief, mental and physical health, and inner peace. As we have discussed earlier, even the common tomato can do some amazing things in terms of communication and adaptivity. What other secrets can we discover in the garden? What other benefits can be obtained from a simple shift in perspective about our relationship toward the plants that we grow?

SOIL

CHAPTER 3
ROOTED IN THE MIND

"To forget how to dig the Earth and to tend the soil is to forget ourselves."

—*Mohandas Gandhi*

How far removed is modern society from nature? Does it influence us? What happens to humanity when it is no longer in direct relationship with the natural world? Does it change us?

The answers to these questions depend on how you view yourself in nature. Are you a part of it, or a stranger within it? Because humans are such mental creatures, our perceptions can greatly alter our behavior and how we react to our environment. When you decide to start a garden, your experience of it can vary based on your approach to the process and the plant life involved. To experience gardening in a way that is spiritually fulfilling, it is important that you are first aware that gardening has a spiritual element to it—that spiritual connection through it is possible. Therefore, we recognize that there is a common tradition of attaching spiritual significance to nature and gardening.

Second, spiritual gardening involves knowing that when you engage in plant care, you are dealing with living things whose well-being and awareness should be considered. Interactions and treatment should be with the best intentions. You should acknowledge that you are engaging with sentient beings with a right to life and expression. Then your enjoyment and use of them becomes tied to the life experience and growing process of the plants just as much as it is to the result. This can add emotional depth to gardening and greater significance to what is observed.

We can now look at a third dimension of spiritual gardening, related to how it impacts you mentally. Subtle psychological benefits can be obtained from gardening. There are reasons that time spent in the garden might sporadically provide mental clarity or inspire gratitude or peacefulness with nature. This has stress-relieving value, which can support your other efforts toward optimal health. With awareness of these effects, you can craft your hobby to have these moments more often. It starts with perspective and knowing your place.

Humans have been conditioned to believe that we are the highest form of life on this planet. We think of ourselves as wholly unique, separate, and, above all, masters of Earth. This conceptualization has proven toxic not only to the environment but also to humanity. Humanocentrism, the literal belief that the world revolves around humans and our actions, has alienated humanity in ways we still may not be aware of.

It is natural to have primary concern for our own species. That is not the problem. Rather, it is the attitude of separateness from the whole that I speak of. Our ancient wisdom traditions did not regard nature this way. Our earliest and safest forms of medicine, like traditional Chinese medicine, Ayurveda, or indigenous herbalism practices, did not heal us by disregarding the environment—quite the opposite, as they uniformly would have had their unique ways of accounting for the influences of the environment on our health.

Routine contact with nature and the elements is often used as a balancing therapy for mental ailments and emotional healing within these disciplines. If we could obtain healing by treating nature as part of ourselves, then what have we gained by taking on a separated perspective? What gifts did we lose in losing sight of the integrative view of nature? How can your garden help you reconnect to these parts of the human experience? Part of what we are experiencing when we garden with a spiritual focus is a softening of the barriers between ourselves and nature. We are incorporating our interest and energy into the process of growing our own food. We are spending more time outdoors. All these aspects of the experience place you within the flow of life and subtly affect your inner feelings of fulfillment and happiness.

Humans, as a species, are dangerously capable of altering their environment, and these changes often have great effects on other living creatures. Irrespective of this, humanity's relationship with nature has gone through stages ranging from reverence to disregard. On one extreme, there are those who live as some of the cultures described in chapter 1, respecting nature's forces to the point of seeing divine significance in her. On the other end of the spectrum, there are those, like those in the global industrial systems, who see the natural world as merely a source of raw materials and use it for their own purposes without regard for its complexities or systems of life.

By respecting the scope of our influence on the environment while understanding our connection to it, we can learn to make more balanced and harmonious choices in regard to our treatment and usage of the planet. The garden can teach us in this way because it relates directly to our life through diet and connects us to the life process of the plants. If your desire is to harmonize with nature, you may want to take an approach that is cooperative. As a part of this natural world, your work with and through it should flow naturally. When you look at your plants and realize that their needs and desires are not that different than your own biological needs, a kind of respect takes shape. Much like yourself, a plant depends on the environment for life, although maybe in a more obvious way.

Mostly, it is your own level of self-awareness that will determine how you treat and process your environment. Were you born into the world, or out of it? This question is at the heart of how we connect with the natural world. Are we unwanted guests on a living planet? Or are we part of the living essence therein? Do humans play a role in the harmony of life on Earth? If so, what is that role? Questions like these have no right or wrong answer. However, I believe that the garden holds the key to unlocking your own truth. Gardening is one of the few human endeavors in which one gets to observe and participate in the life cycle of other beings. It is a time when we get to partner with the natural actions of the Sun and the Moon, and weather, to create. It connects us to nature in real ways, through action, proximity, and diet. Only then can we know the truth that ancient philosopher Chuang Tzu expressed when he said, "Heaven, Earth and I are living together, and all things and I form an inseparable unity."

EGO VS. ENVIRONMENT

At times, we may seem in control of our environment, while at others, we may be at its mercy. A garden places you in close contact with this truth as you meet challenges along the way. Weather, pests, and weeds are just a few small reminders that some of the gardening process is outside of your control. On the other hand, you may reflect after doing your routine maintenance and admire the precision and organization of your garden. The closer one lives in connection with the natural world, the more evident this relationship between your ego and your environment becomes. When showing dominance, the ego feels empowered and capable and therefore moves beyond mere survival into ingenuity and building a comfortable space. However, when nature reminds us of just how small we are, the ego tends to feel overwhelmed and insignificant in relation to the forces of our planet. It seems that this perception is always changing and adapting to the world it observes. This tells us more about ourselves than it speaks to reality.

When you can use mindfulness to register this pendulum of perspective shifting, and work through it by cultivating patience with your garden, you are gaining skills that can carry over into other areas of your mental health. The garden will definitely provide opportunities to work on your ego, because despite your efforts, you can be responsible for only a certain amount of what makes it all happen. A garden is a partnership with nature, and you are not always able to bend the circumstances of the process to your will.

However, the focus here is on you! Your outlook, your conceptualization. How tuned in are you to the power of this planet to sustain all life? Do you understand that just as every living creature on this planet is supported through a complex ecosystem, so are you? Gardening can place us back in touch with the idea that the planet sustains and supports your life. Realizing this truth can relieve anxious feelings of solitude and alienation. Gardening can show you a different perspective—one in which nature yields its blessings, because you are a part of it and worthy of its support. By working in harmony, you and nature are merged in a singular supportive process. It is very healing psychologically and emotionally anytime we encounter support.

This applies to support from the Earth just as it applies to support from the community: By doing my part, I will also be taken care of. When you think of the many factors and coincidental actions that must fall in place even for a single seed to grow to fruition on its own, they are numerous. The right balance of light and water, soil quality, hostility of neighboring plants, invasive insect species, the seed remaining undisturbed long enough to root, the uncertainty of whether the plant will be eaten or damaged during the process—these are all issues that are greatly impacting the probability of life for this plant. Yet, somehow, it still manages to grow. Nature allows it and sees that it is nourished. This kind of support is a natural part of life, and accessible to you as well. Gardening can bring your awareness back to this truth. You do not have to live as if you are separate from the world; rather, you can use your hobby to come back home to it.

>>>>> SEPARATION ANXIETY <<<<<

To change our view of the natural world from that of a dangerous, wild environment to that of a supportive living system, we must first realize the root causes of the belief that we are separate. Much can be said about this in a general sense, but let's bring it closer to home. What role does nature play in your personal life experience? How present is nature for you? If you were born in a rural area or had people in your life who farmed and gardened, this disconnect from nature may not exist for you. You grew up playing and working in nature, dealing closely with the elements, and observing for yourself its wonder and activities. It would be safe to say that your appreciation for animal and plant life is slightly different than that of your urban-centric peers.

However, for many today, urban and suburban living is the norm. This usually does not cut nature out completely, but it does keep it seemingly apart from our day-to-day interactions. In these living conditions, one may go to a park or other designated outdoor spaces to come in contact with nature. However, if you are limited to this form of contact, it is not conducive to gaining a real awareness of how to cooperate with it.

These more modern aspects of human life condition us to regard the natural world as foreign and see ourselves as observers or visitors rather than as participants. We have increasingly created jobs and industries that are dependent on technology and that limit outdoor contact. As we deal with the threat of disease, we continue to sanitize our living spaces, opting for less and less organic contact with the elements. This trend moves society away from knowing our unity with the environment.

It has been a belief among conservationists and nature-oriented people that this has been detrimental to both humanity and Nature. Author E. B. White once remarked, "I would feel more optimistic about a bright future for man if he spent less time proving that he can outwit Nature and more time tasting her sweetness and respecting her seniority."[38] Gardening is an accessible way for us to counteract these trends of moving away from nature.

---

[38] E.B. White, *Letters of E.B. White*, (New York: Harper Perennial Modern Classics, 2007).

SELF-SUSTAINABILITY, SAFETY, AND CONFIDENCE

On the surface, starting a garden may seem small and trivial. However, with experience, you may find that cultivating this skill gives you confidence and security. This feeling does not just come into your life because of the accomplishment of learning something new. That is part of it, for sure, but not necessarily the most important. Rather, it comes from knowing that you can provide for yourself and your family, independent of society. Given the current climate of the food industry, and now even more so with limitations and adjustments of the restaurant business in compliance with germ safety, social distancing, and so on, the food supply chain is a very real concern for some. Those who have grown up with gardening within the culture of their household or communities may not be as affected. These fortunate individuals are familiar with how to cultivate, harvest, and preserve food, with how to live off the land and sustain. But for many, these fears about where and how they will get their food are quickly becoming a reality.

It says a lot about how industrialized society has developed and grown away from the basics of life. While convenient, this food system places the individual person at the mercy of an economically driven industry that doesn't always have the best interest of the customers in mind. Many scandals have come and gone over the years involving food companies, ranging from improper handling and packaging of food to degrading food quality in favor of cost management to poor farming practices and, of course, environmental hazards. Some of these have come with terrible consequences for the public, including sickness, contamination, and even death of customers. Try as some may, it is just not realistic to think that any business will treat your food or health with the same care that you, or even a local farm operation, would. This is a major concern and source of anxiety for some people. If we are what we eat, would it not be more satisfying and safer to eat food that you know the origins of, and to know who handles it before it reaches your mouth?

Let's consider a common scenario of how your food reaches your table. If we look at potatoes, for instance, it may illustrate the point of just how many hands and situations this produce goes through before you eat it. It's possible that some people's anxiety over food is warranted. Hypothetically speaking, a potato is mass-produced on a farm in Idaho. Once it is ready to harvest, workers dig the potato up and sort it out in large quantities (among which some are rotten or otherwise compromised), ship it after a period of holding time by multiple means—sometimes over long distances—deliver it to the grocery store, and shelve it for your perusal. All the while, it is handled by numerous hands, including previous customers, who may have also eyed the produce, that one would hope are sanitary. Not to mention that it is typical for there to still be some dirt or residue of the soil on the potato at the store. Surely, even the harmless benign microbiology of one of these potatoes, let alone those that are potentially harmful, would be interesting.

By contrast, a potato grown in your personal garden would've been handled from seed to table by you, well cared for in the process, and as sanitary as you wanted it to be by the time you ate it. No doubts, no trusting a network of strangers, no concerns about the nutritiousness or quality—all done by you for you and yours. This is deeply comforting and reassuring. To be fully appreciated, it must be experienced, but knowing that you have provided good, clean, healthy food for your loved ones by the work of your own hands is rewarding and builds confidence. In a sense, it is its own kind of wealth.

This feeling of security is a rewarding psychological product of reconnecting with nature. It can bring one back into an understanding of oneself as a member of this planet and citizen of the universe, primarily, and a member of human society, secondarily. When we work with our hands in the soil, feeling the sun kissing our skin, the refreshing waters, and cooling winds, we are experiencing the essential elements of all creation. We are whole, in a sense. Maybe you have never considered it this intensely, seeing it as bothersome or a chore, but the health benefits of these experiences in the garden for our mind and bodies are impressive.

≫≫≫ MONEY DOESN'T GROW ON TREES ≪≪≪

One of the most highly reported causes of stress in the United States is financial insecurity. Norman B. Anderson, former CEO and executive vice president of the American Psychological Association, stated, in the survey *Stress in America: Paying with Our Health*, that "regardless of the economic climate, money and finances have remained the top stressor since our survey began in 2007. Furthermore, this year's survey shows that stress related to financial issues could have a significant impact on Americans' health and well-being."[39] In 2021, with the impact of COVID-19 on the economy, US citizens are feeling even more financial uncertainty and pressure. Those with families and others depending on them must be especially aware of the costs of food consumption.

Now, consider growing most of your produce as high-quality, organic, healthy food with little cost or risk. This allows you to not only maintain the healthiest possible diet but also do so cost-effectively. Gardening, even a small-scale operation, can provide some security in these unsure times. To highlight the relevance of this, the National Gardening Association states that a garden can produce about half a pound of food per square foot.[40] Assuming that you give yourself ample space or use suitable means of vertical and/or space-saving gardening, this could mean saving several hundred dollars per month on your grocery spending.

The ability to work with nature to grow food is a skill that can prove valuable in ways that you may have not previously considered. According to the Consumer Expenditure Survey from the Bureau of Labor Statistics, the average American household forks out $6,759 on food every year, $756 of which goes toward fruits and vegetables.[41] While this is only a fraction of the average food cost, it does add up. When considering that

---

39 "American Psychological Association Survey Shows Money Stress Weighing on Americans' Health Nationwide," American Psychological Association, 2015, https://www.apa.org/news/press/releases/2015/02/money-stress.
40 *National Gardening Survey, 2020 Edition*, Garden Research, 2020, https://.www.gardenresearch.com.
41 Curtis Taylor, "How Gardening Could Save You $600 on Groceries," Money, April 5, 2016, https://money.com/gardening-grocery-savings.

a person can take a DIY approach and produce one's own fruits and vegetables, it seems to be a no-brainer. Gardening can be just as much of a financially motivated activity as it is a healthy diet practice or hobby.

>>>>> GARDEN THERAPY <<<<<

The psychological mind is heavily influenced and, in some ways, shaped by sensual experience. Gardens provide a buffet of natural sensual input, and many people choose to garden simply for the beautiful colors, exotic shapes, and soothing aromatics. Gardeners who place more emphasis on these factors may prefer an herb or flower garden over produce. Even a flower garden can feed the soul. As the Buddha once said, "If we could see the miracle of a single flower clearly, our whole life would change."[42] The underlying wisdom of such a statement pertains to beauty and form of the flower, as well as the miracle of existence, as mentioned before.

Have you ever noticed how one's spirit can be uplifted by merely seeing or smelling a flower? Many have had this experience. There are reasons for this related to the understanding of consciousness. Loretta G. Breuning, author of *Habits of a Happy Brain*, stated in a 2017 article that "bright colors signaled valuable nutrition for our hunter-gatherer ancestors. They balanced their diet by scanning for spots of color. They didn't do it because they knew the chemistry; they did it because dopamine made them feel good."[43]

This primal attraction to the beauty of plant life is so hardwired into us that our bodies physically react to flowers by secreting feel-good chemicals and hormones into our system. Knowing this, gardeners can skillfully affect the emotional health of themselves and others who visit their garden or landscaping. In this same way, one can manipulate moods through the olfactory system. The pleasant smell of flowers, much like their colorful appearance, triggers some ancient neurological link for humans, as they have been used from the very beginnings of society for increased well-being.

---

42 Jack Kornfield, *Buddha's Little Instruction Book*, (Bantam: 1994), 112.
43 Loretta G. Breuning, "Why Flowers Make Us Happy," *Psychology Today*, June 21, 2017

The impact of this information on your gardening hobby can be transformative. Gardening can either directly or indirectly have the following beneficial effects on your mental life:

- Building self-reliance
- Reinforcing oneness with nature
- Increasing self-confidence
- Assuring support from the universe
- Enhancing peaceful moods

These and other gifts are to be encouraged in anyone's life, as they make life more pleasant. These benefits support a healthy outer social life as well as a clearer, more peaceful inner mental space. The thought that natural scenes of flowers and vegetation are healing for the human mind is not a new concept.

At the VU University Medical Center in Amsterdam, a team of researchers headed by Magdalena M. H. E. van den Berg developed data in support of this very concept. These medical scientists recruited sixty students to be exposed to the Montreal Imaging Stress Test (MIST) to analyze their psychological stress levels. Measuring parasympathetic and sympathetic nervous system activity, the team then had these students view scenes of urban green spaces or built spaces to test their psychological recovery time from the stress that they were exposed to. Afterward, van den Berg stated that "the findings of this study point to a predominant role of the parasympathetic nervous system in recovery from stress after exposure to green space." She later commented, "Viewing green scenes may thus be particularly effective in supporting relaxation and recovery after experiencing a stressful period, and thereby could serve as an opportunity for micro-restorative experiences and a promising tool in preventing chronic stress and stress-related diseases."[44]

44 Magdalena M. H. E. van den Berg et al., "Autonomic Nervous System Responses to Viewing Green and Built Settings: Differentiating Between Sympathetic and Parasympathetic Activity," *International Journal of Environmental Research and Public Health* 12, no. 12 (December 14, 2015): 15860–15874.

This is in direct support of traditional holistic wellness systems such as Ayurveda, traditional Chinese medicine, and herbal medicine. Stress is one of the main causes of any disease, but especially the chronic issues. We can deduce that any activity we can do routinely to reduce stress in our lives would be beneficial. Gardening accomplishes this by encouraging physical activity, focus, and exposure to nature's beauty.

In traditional Japanese spirituality, we find the practice of *shinrin-yoku*, or forest bathing, as a way of taking in the atmosphere of the forest for therapy. Much like spending quiet time in your garden, this practice consists of exploration of the forest with a few minutes of mindfulness and introspection. This stress-relieving technique was found to be effective by the research of a team headed by scientist Yuko Tsunetsugu. It was concluded that the "physiological responses suggest that sympathetic nervous activity was suppressed, and parasympathetic nervous activity was enhanced in the forest area." The data collected also showed that the subjective "comfortable," "calm," and "refreshed" feelings were "significantly higher" after time spent in the forest.[45] These findings are not arbitrary. Rather, they lend support to something humanity has been aware of all along: Elements of nature nourish our body, mind, and spirit.

Although your tomato garden may not be a varied botanical wonderland such as a national park or a jungle, it can yield some of these same benefits if focused on and cultivated daily. These mind-balancing aspects of nature can be brought right in your home and used to supplement your other mental health self-care activities. This is only one of the ways that a spiritual gardening practice can support your growth as a conscious being.

---

[45] Yuku Tsunetsugu et al., "Physiological Effects of Shinrin-Yoku (Taking in the Atmosphere of the Forest) in an Old-Growth Broadleaf Forest in Yamagata Prefecture, Japan," *Journal of Physiological Anthropology* 26, no. 2 (March 2007): 135–142.

CHAPTER 4

GROWING PAINS

"The nation that destroys its soil destroys itself."
—*Franklin Delano Roosevelt*

We really should marvel at the beauty and efficiency of life on this planet, the result of the right balance of elements and conditions for life to not only survive but also thrive within every square inch of its surface and depths—life big and small, plant, fungal, animal, bacterial, microbial, viral, human, amphibian, aquatic, terrestrial, life on top of life on top of life. Suffice it to say that this planetary state of well-being is delicate and transient.

During the past couple of decades, the negative effects of factory farming and the food industry have become more public. What started as fringe theories and political hearsay became more mainstream as reports from both the medical and scientific communities grew in support of further investigation into the issues. Currently, many experts see our society at a crisis point regarding this relationship between our planet and our food consumption.

This has grown to a level of importance that warrants a serious global effort for change. One area of global concern is deforestation. All over the world, our forests have been disappearing in the wake of food- and plant-producing industries. Cattle farming, soy production, and other forms of monocropping have done some serious harm to the environment, and some conservationists even warn that certain effects are already irreversible. Unfortunately, there are many sides to these issues, and progress has been slow. On an individual scale, we can all do the small things: Actions like recycling and reuse of materials, reduction of waste, conservation of resources, diet alternatives, and lowering carbon emissions are all contributing to healing the planet.

Gardening is one such practice we all can do to help. You may have never considered your garden to be an investment in environmental health, but in every sense, it truly is. The awesome thing about gardening is that you get direct benefit and experience that is enjoyable and transformative for its own sake. In the previous chapter, we spoke about how the garden can be beneficial as a food source and provide peace of mind. Now, let us add to these sentiments by including the ways in which it can help heal the world.

As of this moment, the food industry is in an environmental mess. Before judging it for this state of affairs, out of fairness, some things must be considered. For starters, the food industry is exactly what it is: the industry of food. In many ways, food producers are, themselves, a product of the ecosystem around food. On average, American society makes poor decisions in portions and choices of food. This has been a national concern for decades, with only faint glimmers of change on the horizon. To say that more people are health conscious today than years before would be accurate. However, we still have a long road ahead in building a wellness-focused society.

The problems the food industry faces come down to one key factor of business: the principle of supply and demand. When businesses are built around supplying a necessary resource like food, it can only be assumed that they will meet disaster and pitfalls. For starters, food, by nature, is a finite resource. Despite the Earth's bounty, eventually, there just aren't going to be any more coconuts on the tree or enough livestock being born. Nature is generous and plentiful, but it is also patient and balancing, taking time to develop the nutrients we take in. A sane creature will eat only what it needs to sustain itself and move on. However, humanity has developed some very unhealthy relationships with food.

This isn't even the problem—how you eat and what you eat is, and should be, personal. The problem lies in that we have built an entire culture around eating a certain way, and this culture affects billions of people. As a business, these food conglomerates must do their best to keep up with these desires. Even the most well-meaning and ethical business will cut corners wherever possible. This is only logical in most industries, but when we consider the industry of food, it becomes an uncomfortable fact. No one likes to think of the budget cuts, low ethical practices, or sanitation and logistic shortcuts that go into the food you're eating. When it comes to the environment, unfortunately, ecological concerns are often an afterthought. In fact, it wasn't until a few short decades ago that the environment became such an important factor in how we source our foods. Before these problems can be tackled with intelligence, society must become fully aware of what the real challenges are.

Some of the most glaring ecological issues of the food industry are related to land distribution. Never in human history has so much of the surface of the planet been allocated to agriculture. As humanity swells in population, with no feasible or ethical way of slowing it down, we are simultaneously dedicating more and more land to livestock and monocropping. In research published by the Food and Agriculture Organization of the United Nations, it was found that half of all habitable land on the surface of planet Earth is used for agriculture![46] Half! That means our wild areas, forests, and even human dwellings are included in the other half, which is only 29 percent of the planet.

The long and short of it is that there's not as much land on Earth as it may appear. Of that land, only a small percentage of it is livable, and to support our food demands, we must use half of that habitable land. This shows a great disparity in how we are handling the food

[46] Earl C. Ellis et al., "Anthropogenic Transformation of the Biomes, 1700 to 2000," *Global Ecology and Biogeography* 19, no. 5 (2010): 589–606.

business and its distribution. What is even more depressing is that most of this agricultural land isn't producing the best foods for us. Seventy-seven percent of this land around the globe is dedicated to raising livestock.[47] While eating meat may be a personal choice, it shows an imbalance in our overall diet, when so much energy and resources go toward livestock. It is no wonder that this is not a sustainable model.

Similarly, the practice of monocropping has some fundamental flaws in its attitude toward the environment. Monocropping is the agricultural practice of dedicating an entire farming space to one cash crop—soy, corn, and so on. On the surface, this may seem harmless. However, farmers all over the globe are clearing valuable biodiverse lands and forests in order to do so. Consider that even as you read this, hundreds of acres of undiscovered food and medicine are disappearing from our world so that we can have more steaks and corn syrup. It's quite sickening to any true nature lover. The insensitive way in which we are exploiting our planet is bound to come back on us if we do not act with awareness.

This is not a condemnation of the food producers. There are those working hard to try to make a difference. Sadly, in many cases, the farmers can't afford to care. They are trying to make a living

---

[47] Joseph Poore and Thomas Nemecek, "Reducing Food's Environmental Impacts Through Producers and Consumers," *Science* 360, no. 6392 (2018): 987–992.

and competing with a fast-moving industry. The entire scenario is indicative of a sickness within humanity. We have lost the true value of our natural world and our foods.

Gardening is a way for people to balance these negatives. If personal gardening became more of a fixture in mainstream society, it would mean less strain on the food industry and healthier food consumption overall. For your part, you can be responsible only for your own actions, but growing a garden and sharing the experience with others can only be positive. We enhance this even further when we experience gardening with more depth.

Another big focus of concern over the food industry is carbon emissions. This has been a hot topic ever since it was discovered that certain actions are depleting our ozone layer. Even though most of the world sprang into action, the food industry continued to fly under the radar as one of the biggest contributors to the problem. It wasn't until recently that environmentalists began to take a serious look at how the food industry affects the air quality of the planet. Carbon emissions are not something the average person would probably associate with cattle ranching or farming.

Nevertheless, the information on greenhouse gases caused by the agriculture industry is alarming. Data published in *Science* magazine in 2018 from the research of Joseph Poore and Thomas Nemecek shows that 26 percent of all greenhouse emissions are due to the food industry. The breakdown of that figure is even more revealing. Of course, in any business that involves distribution, there will be emissions from transportation, packaging, and processing. The research found 18 percent of the total emissions from food to be due to these factors, comparable to the costs found in other industries. What is astounding and problematic to our environment is the 31 percent of emissions that comes from the care, maintenance, and housing of animals that are used for food. Another 6 percent is caused by the process of feeding these animals until they are slaughtered.[48]

---

48 Ibid.

One may not consider the problems that this creates. The planet, like any other biological system, maintains its own sense of balance. What we are doing to the planet through current methods is upsetting the balance. We are doing something unnatural through factory farming. Between other predators and the processes of a natural life cycle, cows and other livestock would not exist in the numbers that they do in our system. They would not breed nearly as much, nor would they have the necessary access to food to sustain such a population. Nature balances all life on this planet in this way. Humanity has enough ingenuity and technology to fight against many of these population checks, but we are not exempt by any means. If we had to pick and forage whatever nature gave us, as our ancestors did, and had nothing else to eat, our population figures would quickly fall.

Obviously, it is a great thing that humanity has figured out how to produce enough food for our species. However, we have overdone it and not done it responsibly. And when we add this many more animals to the environment without some sort of check other than the economy, it is irresponsible. Cattle, for instance, naturally produce methane gas as part of their digestive process. Large amounts of methane are toxic to humans and most life on this planet, not to mention that it is a greenhouse gas. In order to support the beef-loving appetites of humanity, farmers all over the world are pumping out cows as quickly as they can. That means we have that much more methane in the atmosphere than we should organically.

This particular problem is one of the most relevant because of its multilayered damage to the ecosystem, but every animal product that is being factory farmed has its own version of this. Even fisheries and seafood harvesting are major contributors to these carbon-emission figures, dispelling the myth that the beef industry is the main problem. All of this takes energy; all of it produces waste. Much of that waste is excessive and not healthy for the planet. Period. But what to do?

What do we do about the tragic loss of the land used for these food-industry operations? Regardless of the potential discoveries that they can provide, these massive areas are cut down and burned to make way for the crops that humanity's consumer market deems are most valuable. This wipes out numerous numbers of species of plants and animals. When we lose members of the plant kingdom, we are losing something extremely valuable to the well-being of the entire planet: producers of breathable air.

In order to live, every bit of plant life on this planet is taking in the carbon dioxide that we breathe out. Every plant is breathing out your next breath, and in this way acts as an extension of your very lungs. This isn't just a metaphor; it is literally the way air is circulated and shared on this planet among living beings. So, what happens when we simultaneously destroy these oxygen-producing plants and pump more pollutant air into the atmosphere? One doesn't have to be an ecologist to know that a system like this is doomed to fail.

Many around the globe have expressed concern about this system, and solutions are being formulated. Several common factors can be found in any feasible solution:

- Repopulation and conservation of plant life
- Systemic changes in diet and perspectives on food
- Getting food from local sources
- Cultivating ecological awareness

Other important issues must also be handled, but these four focuses are easily solved through gardening. By gardening, you are cultivating more plant life in your local environment, increasing your access to organic, nutritious produce, and providing your own food source, all while doing your small part to reduce humanity's carbon footprint. Not too shabby, gardener! It may not be an obvious contribution, but gardening is a valuable tool toward environmental sustainability.

The current food industry was created to mass-produce food products for society. Hence, it is only logical that any movement toward counteracting the mass-producing part of the equation will only help. Anytime people can grow vegetables, fruits, and herbs in their backyard, that is a little less travel, financial cost, space, and energy spent on getting the food you desire to your dinner table. It may seem small, but really, consider how much you and your family consume in a year. Even if one takes an every-little-bit-counts approach, a garden is beneficial.

Of course, there are key crops and products that people would still rely on the industry for, but imagine how much better it would be overall if more people gardened. The food in your routine diet would be healthier and more nutritious, less pesticide and fewer chemicals would be needed, fewer wildlands would have to be cut and maintained for food production, and individually, each person would save a significant amount of money. This approach wouldn't cut out the industry altogether, nor should it, but it could provide some much-needed balance. A garden is more than just a plot of cultivated soil. It is an experience, an attitude toward life, and if enough were to discover its gifts, gardening could be a tool for a brighter future.

Part of spiritual understanding is knowing that what you do and experience is connected to everything else—having a belief that even the simplest acts, when done with intention, can have big effects. The act of gardening is no different. Remain open to its wisdom, and listen from within as you experience and test the techniques found here. You may come to find that the impact it has on you and those around you grows. It is this kind of growth that can multiply and shake up the culture of environmental damage and overuse that we have grown accustomed to. The garden can provide a way of unplugging from this system of negative consequences and karma that we call the food industry.

The garden can be many things. The more your heart is open to its secrets, the more the garden's sweetness infuses into every part of you. Its flowers of stillness, reflection, calm, and loving patience will bloom in other aspects of your life. I have taken you down this road in order to give you some grounding in the concepts involved in a spiritual gardening practice. The information provided from this point on serves to build on a basic understanding and openness to these ideas.

⟫⟫⟫ GROUNDING MEDITATION ⟪⟪⟪

For this meditation, we will start as we did before, by getting comfortable and relaxing. (This meditation is best practiced outdoors where you can touch the soil, but if you are indoors, this is fine.) Once you have found your happy still place, close your eyes. Begin with a fully pressed exhalation, using your diaphragm to push all the air from your body. Inhale air slowly by calmly relaxing your stomach muscles, as though you were allowing it to enter rather than pulling it in with your chest. Breathe like this for a few minutes, eyes closed.

Release the tension in your body with each breath cycle, starting at your head and making your way down to your feet. Let your mind play and yell all it wants; simply stay with the breath and observe. Ease your muscles and mind, and become aware of the automated function of your thoughts and sensations. Let them do their own thing as you observe without engagement. Thoughts come and go, but you are not them. Rather, you are the awareness of the thoughts. Keep focusing on your breath and remain in your stillness and relaxation. Let's breathe deep like this for five to seven cycles. Let go of anything else that may come into your attention. Nothing that you did before this matters, and neither does what you will do next. Be here, now.

Once you have done a few minutes of deep breathing, shift your focus to the ground beneath you. Remaining still, with eyes closed, notice the firmness and solidity underneath you. Whether you are sitting or lying down, feel the Earth. If you are sitting in a chair, notice that even this is stable because of its contact with the ground. You are supported, lifted by the very Earth under you. If it helps and is reachable, feel the ground. Do not be distracted by the shift in motion. Just reach and feel. Feel through the floor, knowing that ultimately, the

Earth is supporting it. This precious Earth, made of dirt and stone, upholds all the life of this planet. Even the oceans lie on top of the ground far beneath its surface.

This ground provides the foundation for all things on this planet. In this moment, we are just making ourselves aware of its ever-present, supportive nature. Feel this sentiment, feel its energy, recognize the stability that we take for granted all the time. You are connected to the Earth; you are rooted and nourished by its energy.

As you think over these things, remain still and stay with your breath. Has your breathing changed? Is it deeper, or more shallow? Simply observe and return to the rhythm of engaging your diaphragm. Once you feel settled and relaxed into this experience, refocus your awareness on your contact with the Earth. Feel your energy reach down to it as the Earth presses against you. Realize this connection between your body and the Earth. Ground yourself in this relationship. Give loving energy back to it, as if to embrace, serve, and protect it. Be in tune with this reciprocal support system.

Now, let's introduce a new meditative practice. While staying aware of your contact with the ground, audibly hum the sound "*aum*." Keep your mouth and eyes closed while feeling this vibration throughout your body. Notice the direction that this vibration travels throughout your being. Feel it move up or down, or even outward from your center. Stretch the vibration out as long as you can without distracting too much from your inner stillness.

Remember, this is not a task to be performed; instead, let it be a natural part of the experience. "*Auuuuuuuummmmmmmmmmm.*" Say it mentally as your vocal cords vibrate the sound inwardly. Come from the diaphragm, humming as clearly and powerfully as you can while being mindful not to excite yourself. Stay calm; stay grounded. Do this for a few breaths. Feel the vibration go down into the ground underneath you. Feel it bounce back up into you. Pay attention to this motion. Notice the sensation of it. Enjoy the feeling it gives you, and remain still otherwise.

Do this for as long as you'd like, but be sure to give it at least seven rounds. When you have felt this fully and are ready, return to silently breathing. Relax in the moment, and let yourself bathe in the reverberations of this energy. Be aware of how your body feels. Notice the peace of mind you are experiencing. This is a result of communing with the Earth, and it is always available to you. This ground, even in all its hardness and solidity, is full of life energy. This ground holds and nourishes the seeds of life. And when it is appropriate, the Earth opens and gives way to a brand-new expression. In this moment, you are this life energy! You are a part of it; you can feel it. And now you have connected to it.

Before ending this meditation, silently thank the Earth for this, and for so much more that it does for you and all life on this planet. Genuinely say, "Thank you" within your heart for this great gift of support and stability that is often taken for granted. When you have done this to your satisfaction, release the breath and slowly open your eyes.

CHAPTER 5
SOUL IN THE SOIL
MEDITATION IN THE GARDEN

"Now I see the secret of making the best person: It is to grow in the open air and to eat and sleep with the earth."

—*Walt Whitman*

As the birthplace of humanity, both philosophically and literally, the bountiful garden holds many untold mysteries and wonders. Imagine what the first humans must have thought as they looked out at an abundant, lush, colorful scene. Through trial and error, or some ephemeral guidance, humanity began to understand which plants were useful as food, which ones were medicinal, and which ones were harmful. According to many shamanic traditions, the spirit world guided humanity from striving to survive in this landscape to flourishing, and eventually dominating their environment. This skilled manipulation and usage had to come from a deeper level of consciousness. Even if accomplished through scientific means, these early humans would have had to spend a lot of time in study and contemplation on the nature of these plant beings.

Eventually, there emerged a class of men and women who made it their life's work to understand the plant kingdom. Some called them priests and priestesses; others knew them as medicine men and women, gurus, witches and warlocks, and the like. All over the world, at various stages, there have been signs of this development. These were women and men who were compelled to connect with the natural world, sometimes even in exile from the rest of the community, in order to know its secrets and unify with it.

What we learn from this is that a natural need arises for this kind of specialization. When living in harmony with the natural environment, one must have understanding. No matter what one believes to be the source of this information, humanity has been inspired, countless times over, to go into the wild for sustenance, guidance, and health concerns. With the discovery of gardening came the ability to control and sustain these blessings from the plant kingdom. No longer was wild foraging or gathering necessary. Instead, the community was able to obtain its food and medicine within settled, protected lands. This gave rise to mercantile exchange and the formation of the village social structure, by way of creating a centralized plant-cultivation effort for the group.

Quite often, the herbalist also wore the hat of chief chef and medicine person, due to the connection between the two skills. While some information would have been commonly known, these herbal specialists would have been the foremost authorities on plants in these earliest stages of human development. As gardening grew as a practice and became more personalized to each home, this skill needed to be shared with others so that each family subgroup would have its own herbalist. Whether this responsibility fell on one member or was a shared task was probably determined culturally. Regardless, these were the beginnings of the modern-day practice of gardening.

All at once, the tribal group was able to access food without relying so heavily on moving about. The family center was born, as people now had a centralized means of sustaining themselves. To this very day, many smaller communities have a farm or garden to depend on, either as individual households or as a communal space. This has been very advantageous for humanity, though the modern world eventually evolved markets and grocery stores to mostly replace the need for a home garden. Today, the garden is more of a hobby or a personal choice than a necessity. Yet, we still rely on it.

Along the way, however, something else began to take shape. As these herbalists spent enormous amounts of time in nature or in their own crafted gardens, a type of relationship came about. These early herbalists were able to access other layers of consciousness and attunement with their environment. Spiritual healing and assistance came while doing this work. Deeper levels of understanding developed, and some would even claim communication with the plant kingdom. Shamans, devoid of any formal training or school, formed whole apothecaries of medicine for a range of ailments, all through spiritual or intuitive guidance. How was this so?

Undoubtedly, food was a major, if not prime, motivation for gardening in the beginning. However, if we look at the various expressions of specialization that this evolved into around the world, one must see that some deeper drive was present. Ayurveda, the ancient Indian science of life, is the basis for many of the techniques found in this book. Its inclusion is due to the synergistic nature of its philosophies and those found globally that encourage natural healthy living. This practice survives today as a 5,000-year-old detailed, documented medical science that relies heavily on herbalism and environmental unity. It is not the only one of its kind. Indeed, one could find a similar understanding of the herbal content and food sources of the natural environment in most early developed communities of the world. As stated before, it would have been a prehistoric necessity for the survival of any community of humans.

However, Ayurveda holds a special place and honor, since the people of India have allowed it to survive intact as it was practiced thousands of years ago. The amount of detailed recording and research dedicated to this science for centuries and the importance it has held in the daily life of the people are probably responsible factors for this preservation, as Ayurveda has been uniquely treasured within the Vedic culture of India. Also worthy of mention are the practices of traditional Chinese medicine, which in a similar way have been preserved and continue to be in use today.

Records of the advanced medical sciences of other great civilizations of antiquity are lost to history or have been absorbed into other surviving practices. How much wisdom have we lost from societies that did not emphasize this kind of detailed record keeping or were otherwise relegated to the lost sands of time? Surely, human beings all over the world had to develop a keen understanding of the environment around them. As this understanding was allowed to continuously grow into lineages and schools, this would have evolved into sciences and held greater societal significance.

In the case of Ayurveda, we get a unique gift of knowledge that would have been understood to varying degrees by much of humanity. Central tenets like living in harmony with the environment and its seasons, respectful interaction with nature, understanding of self and the universe in a microcosmic and macrocosmic framework, and acknowledgment of universal consciousness or intelligent natural harmony would have been commonly held across the spectrum of humanity, even among the uneducated. These ideas can be found the world over because they are primal understandings of the human experience. This kind of powerful yet simple philosophy about life started with those amazing women and men who chose to devote their lives and energy to communing with the plant world.

It is true that many cultures across the world, especially those of Central and South America, used certain plants and their by-products to access these higher realms. However, even this was done with such respect and precision that one cannot just write it off as tripping out in the jungle and stumbling on medicinal uses. Shamans often speak of communicating with otherworldly beings or the plants themselves and receiving instructions while under the influence of these substances. Since this is a matter of polarized opinions, we won't delve too far into the use of hallucinogens.

The most fascinating and powerful outcome of this shamanic way of life is the natural means discovered. Activities such as trancelike dance ceremonies, meditation, chanting, and sacrifices were done in nature to appease the spirits of nature. Also, many people turned to nature for solitude, contemplation, and wanderlust as a way of clearing the mind and opening the spirit. Instances of spiritual retreat into nature can be found in various religious texts. While some speak specifically of activities or rituals performed in the wild, all point the way to simply losing oneself. All serve the purpose of recalibrating the human being, mind, body, and spirit to the natural vibrations of the environment.

In this part of our journey, we are going deeper into some of these nature-based spiritual practices and how you can make use of them in your personal life. The most important of these is meditation. Those familiar with meditation may discover the power of incorporating nature into their practice, while those who are not might just find themselves a key to unlocking their potential in new ways.

For beginners, meditation can seem a bit daunting. Most do not feel as if they can sit still long enough to get anything out of meditation. Nothing can be further from the truth, but one must experience it to know this. You may have noticed that within each section of this book, there are meditations for you to try. If you are one who has difficulty finding inner stillness, or are just new to the practice, you may find this approach easier. Also, guided meditations, recorded or in person, with someone more experienced may help. It is with this in mind that you are invited to try meditating with your plants. Very few, if any other, living beings on the planet have mastered stillness in the way that plants have as they grow and change before our very eyes, yet are still and serene enough to do so almost magically! This describes a plant's activity, but it can also be a part of

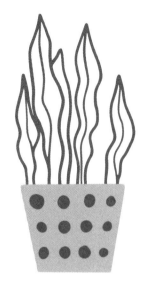

how you move through life. Meditation can help bring the metaphoric and literal truth of this to light.

Meditation has been used as a tool to access our inner dimensions since the beginnings of humanity. Intentional stillness, silence, and observation can open up the mind and body to receive and fully process the influx of energy that one constantly receives and uses in waking life. Though there are many techniques, all meditation essentially serves the purpose of quieting the mind. In moments experienced as pure awareness, the human consciousness is free of the usual baggage of the ego. This is not only pleasurable but also clarifying to the entire system.

The great wisdom traditions often spoke of meditation as the main technique to free the self of bondage—to liberate one's mind and tune into the heart. As explained in the Chandogya Upanishad, "Meditation, indeed, is greater than the mind. The earth, as it were, meditates. The atmosphere, as it were, meditates. Heaven, as it were, meditates. The waters, as it were, meditate. The mountains, as it were, meditate. Both men and gods, as it were, meditate. He who worships God [Brahman] as meditation, as far as meditation extends, so far does he gain the power to act as he wills."[49]

This concept of universal attunement is common in ancient beliefs. Aside from all the various styles of meditation, many rituals and practices from all over the world were designed to accomplish the same goals. From Islamic culture, we get the concept of *taffakur*, or reflection, in which practicing Muslims are intended to spend time in stillness reflecting over their actions, thoughts, and choices and their dedication to their faith. From Africa, we still have remnants of the Kemetic spiritual systems of ancient Egypt and Nubia, which display knowledge and use of meditation and Yogic practices. In the Celtic traditions of Europe, we find meditation, especially in nature, as a common practice and way of spiritual upliftment.

---

49 Swami Lokeswarananda, *Chandogya Upandisha*, (West Bengal, India: Ramakrishna Math, 1998).

While most modern understanding of meditation comes from the Vedic and Tantric systems of ancient India or the Buddhist and Daoist traditions of the Far East, it should be understood that all of humanity can claim some form of it. Meditation is healthy and perhaps vital to a fully functioning, balanced human being. There are even observations in meditating households of pets getting in on the Zen. As the Vedic scripture explains, all is meditating. So, what is going on with people twisting up their fingers and sitting cross-legged? Why is there so much ritual around some meditation techniques? Why do people chant and use long phrases to meditate if it is so simple?

To understand how meditation works, we must look at the human being as consciousness, first and foremost, with the body and mind playing their subsequent roles as expressions of this consciousness. This concept is central to all the sciences originating from Vedic philosophy, including Ayurveda and Yoga. To see your true self as consciousness is to free yourself of the limitations and programming inherent within the mind-body complex. As consciousness, human beings witness and process all the thoughts, sensations, and actions of their persons. Consciousness is the life itself, supported by prana, and entangled within the play of the elements, or the physical world. It is this consciousness that constitutes the "I am" principle in living beings, and therefore gives rise to the ego, the mind, and body-centered identification. Consciousness is the great mystery and support of all life.

Reaching this understanding as one's personal reality is the goal of many Vedic schools of thought, as well as those passed down through the Yogic traditions. As Swami Prabhavananda said in his translation of the Kena Upanishad, "That which is not comprehended by the mind but by which the mind comprehends—know that . . . ."[50] It is to this end that meditation is applied. Meditation helps one to cultivate space within, between the mind and the true consciousness. This ability to silently witness the mind and body's activities with detachment opens new dimensions within a person. Departing from

---

50 "The Kena Upanishad in English," Hinduwebsite.com, 2000, https://www.hinduwebsite.com/kena.asp.

any religious significance of meditation, it is the health benefits that come through this practice that are most enticing.

Meditation goes a long way toward making an individual less reactive to life. The stress, emotional entanglements, traumas, and guilt associated with the mind can be bypassed, and life can be lived, as it is, as manifested truth. To the modern mind, life is all about doing, accomplishing, conquering, and so on, but these are very ego-based motivations. What is gained from meditation is a release of these bindings. Since the human being is composed of several layers of awareness, this release of mental stress and obligation has benefits that range from physical to mental and emotional healing.

Claims that meditation can help health conditions like high blood pressure, irritable bowel syndrome, ulcerative colitis, chronic stress syndrome, anxiety disorders, and depression are scientifically supported and well documented. In a scientific study on the effects of meditation on the cardiovascular and nervous systems, published in *Frontiers in Human Neuroscience* and supported by the Chopra Center, scientists stated, "We were able to show that meditation led to significant, measurable EEG changes even in individuals just beginning a meditation practice. . . . Our most novel and reliable finding however was that meditation was associated with a small but statistically significant decrease in blood pressure in a normotensive population."[51]

In the scientific journal *Translational Psychiatry*, Rudolph Tanzi, the Joseph P. and Rose F. Kennedy Professor of Neurology at Harvard University, and director of the Genetics and Aging Research Unit at Massachusetts General Hospital, said of meditation, "Based on our results, the benefit we experience from meditation isn't strictly psychological; there is a clear and quantifiable change in how our bodies function. . . . Meditation is one of the ways to engage in restorative activities that may provide relief for our immune systems, easing the day-to-day stress of a body constantly trying to protect itself."[52]

---

51 Steven R. Steinhubl et al., "Cardiovascular and Nervous System Changes During Meditation," *Frontiers in Human Neuroscience* 9 (2015): 145.
52 Elissa S. Epel et al., "Meditation and Vacation Effects Impact Disease-Associated Molecular Phenotypes," *Translational Psychiatry* 6, no. 8 (August 30, 2016): e880.

Many of today's leading universities are dedicating time and research to this subject in hopes of understanding how and why it works. Thankfully, the individual meditator does not have to prove anything scientifically. It is only necessary to experience the practice yourself to be convinced of its benefits. Without attempting to engage the entire spectrum of ways to meditate, the focus here will be on some easily accessible and simple forms of practice.

At its core, meditation is just getting still and centered in mind, body, and spirit. Therefore, some of the most effective means of meditation are the simplest. Getting into a comfortable position, closing your eyes, and relaxing through focus on the breath or some other repetitive action—this is the essence of any meditation. As much as can be said about the experience itself, these are the key elements found in virtually any meditative process. Some forms may involve chanting, singing bowls, chimes, music, or some other sound effect. Some may involve incense and aromatics. Others include reading of spiritual literature. However, they all pull the individual into a deeply relaxed mental and physical state where one checks out from the mind's activity and experiences oneself in egoless awareness.

If there is one thing that nature is extremely good at, it is pulling human beings away from their egos. Even a simple, quiet walk through a park can open the mind and release pent-up energy. Proximity with the natural elements of water and fire also seems to soften one's social barriers and relax the stress response in people. Ayurveda explains this—it has to do with the attunement of our inner elements with the outer elements. Like recharging a battery, or tuning to a frequency, humanity is renewed by the physical elemental world. When one can marry the power of meditation with the universal charge station of the natural world, great experiences and benefits can manifest. There is a reason great spiritual masters all over the world have always gone to the wilderness to tap into their truths. There is a reason that moments of insight and deep understanding visit humans while in nature. And this reason is accessible and worthy of investigation.

According to ancient wisdom traditions, the human being as a total life expression is not separate from the environment. Some schools of thought, like Advaita Vedanta from the Vedic traditions, take this idea more literally than others, encouraging followers to see the entire world, including other people, as part of their own being. This is easier for some to accept than others, but it is definitely foreign to modern Westernized thought.

However, when it comes to the natural world, the significance of this concept cannot be overlooked and is much more digestible. Your own body is a composition of the foods you have eaten throughout your life, the experiences you have had over your lifetime, and the results your body produced in reaction to these inputs. While the body is far more complicated in its functioning, the basic physical matter of it is simply this: Cells build from the nutrients they receive from the food you eat, giving rise to the concept that you are what you eat.

Traditions like Ayurveda teach us that the elements are universal and present in all things, including your food. So, in this way, your body has all the five elements from the outside world incorporated into its makeup. Following this understanding, those inner elements are constantly changing and frequently will go out of balance. According to Ayurveda, this is when our health suffers. Most of the work in these holistic disciplines centers around bringing the person's elemental composition back into balance.

While they all may have their own specialized means of accomplishing this, any holistic wellness discipline will at some point require access to the natural elements. It is this inner and outer balance that can be felt as mental and spiritual experience as well. In fact, spiritual realization is not considered separate from physical and mental health functioning; all must be aligned and in balance. Nature helps human beings to easily gain this balance. When one goes to the natural world to open spiritual dimensions, it increases the efficacy of these experiences organically and places us back in touch with our true nature.

The garden, no matter how small, is a little piece of our natural world. In the care of a garden space, or even a singular plant, one encounters all the elements. In any gardening experience, you will always have the following factors to consider:

- Fire = sunlight (exposure/temperature control)
- Water = nourishment of plant
- Air = air quality and flow
- Space = placement and surroundings
- Earth = soil (quality, aeration, content)

These considerations are not just to improve the quality of the plant's life. They also place you in daily contact with these elements, which is great for your being, according to Ayurveda. Being in regular contact with the universal elements is especially important for those who live in urban centers and do not have easy access to the great outdoors.

The great thing about connecting these elements with meditation is that it helps the person center and ground themselves much more easily. The assistance of nature in your process will mostly be felt in your body. The sights, smells, and feeling of being out in nature, the fresh air, and sunlight—all these naturally add beneficial emotions and sensations to the experience. This can be explained through Ayurveda as the balancing of your doshas, the interrelated groupings of the five elements, and that Sanskrit word is often used to describe the imbalance of these elements.

There will be a lot more discussion of doshas in chapter 10. For now, it is necessary only to understand that the element content of your body and the outside world is constantly moving, changing, and adapting. This often creates imbalances. Most are minor, temporary, and not even noticed, while a prolonged imbalance can create disease and generally have a negative impact on your well-being. Ayurveda teaches us that one can create one's own balance or imbalance by the choices one makes, particularly in diet and habitual behaviors. The concept follows that by being aware of the presence of the five elements in all things, one can use the elemental content of one's surroundings, food, drink, and so on to add or counter the imbalances of one's mind and body.

Nature, the home of these elements, therefore, will provide the best source for finding balance. When this balance is achieved, it is not only healthy for the individual but also pleasant. Because it feels good and is refreshing to the body, one's mind and spirit are less bound to the physical world in those moments. The connection between your inner elements and those of the outer world brings a settled feeling while you go inward and observe the mind's activity. This is the gift of meditation in nature. The garden offers us a tamed, controlled, and accessible version of this that one can easily incorporate into one's life.

By using your gardening time for meditation, you can share in some of the magical experiences felt by those early shamans and medicine people of ancient cultures. It is not some fantastic ability that allowed these people to understand the plant world the way they did. All one must do is show up and be open. When you intentionally connect with nature for spiritual or mental upliftment, Mother Earth will do most of the work for you. Just being out in it can instantly bring insight and clarity, pleasantness, and energy.

As you are caring for your garden, try spending a few minutes in quiet reflection, gratitude, and receptivity. Purposefully take your stress and problems into the garden with the intention of releasing them or finding solutions. Understand that your garden is not just a way of getting food, but also your own personal piece of nature. One can approach it the same way you would hike or camp in order to clear your mind. It may seem less obvious because the garden is controlled and/or near the home, and not the location of some wilderness trek, but truthfully, all the same elements are there for your benefit. Before working or harvesting, just be. Breathe deeply and be aware of the gift of your garden and your presence in it. Connect with the surrounding energy of the space you have created.

When we meditate, there is a natural alignment and absorption of the energy within and around us. This is one of the reasons the difference of meditation around your healthy, prana-rich plants can be felt consciously. Did you know that it has been proven that your plants feel that too? In a study published in 2001 in the *American Journal of Chinese Medicine*, researchers Max Haid and Shankar Huprikar found that praying on the water supplied to the plants caused significant growth differences.[53]

This experiment was done on green peas, a common garden plant, not some exotic tropical plant. If it can be proven through science that meditation and prayer will help your plants grow healthier, might it be acceptable that there is something to all this? This is the registration of spiritual energy within a conscious being. For all involved, there is a different level of peace. There is an openness and unity felt, especially when in solitude, that one does not necessarily achieve in other settings.

Though it may be subtle, your houseplants or garden can provide a piece of this in your life. There is something pure and refreshing about caring for plants, whether they are being raised for food or enjoyment. Even indoor herbs or houseplants add this peaceful quality to a home. This can be felt and seen without meditation or any spiritual elements. To a child or an imaginative adult, the garden can become a magical environment—so full of life and activity, colorful and intriguing, a world unto itself.

If you were lucky enough to be able to explore a garden, farm, greenhouse, or the like as a child, maybe you can recall these feelings. One could easily get lost, even in the memory of these experiences. This is the power of the natural world over the human spirit. Even though your granny's flower garden or strawberry patch was cultivated, it still was a way of getting in close proximity with nature. It still involved being in the dirt, smelling the fresh aromas, seeing the vibrant colors, and tasting the nutrient-rich, organic goodness.

Do you remember the first time you smelled a tomato plant as you passed by? What about the refreshing scent of cilantro? How did the soil feel in your hands or feet? How did it smell? Do these thoughts bring emotions or memories with them as you call them up? If you are one who has been fortunate enough to have such experiences, just the mention of these garden qualities should stir something in you. This is evidence of the power of this attraction to and affinity for nature.

---

53 M. Haid and S. Huprikar, "Modulation of Germination and Growth of Plants by Meditation," *American Journal of Chinese Medicine* 29, no. 3–4. (2001): 393–401.

The principle by which this works is called neuroassociative conditioning, the brain's ability and tendency to connect sensual stimuli with impactful experiences in our memories. This brain behavior allows us to consciously reprogram or otherwise use our outer world to heal and enhance ourselves. Relevant uses for this involve aromatherapy, touch therapy, and mindfulness. Just as the previous sensual-memory questions might have had an inner effect, one can create intentional experiences that will impact you at times when it is needed.

For example, if you were to meditate every morning in your garden next to aromatic herbs, such as lavender or chamomile, you would undoubtedly associate a sense of sweetness and tranquility with those scents. These scents naturally produce this effect and would only enhance the power of this experience. After some time of making this a routine—say, two to three weeks—this connection between the smell of the herbs and these peaceful emotions would be pretty well cemented in your consciousness. This is not to mention the actual meditative experiences and whatever benefits, insights, or impact they may add.

The gift of using this meditative technique is that one can later purposefully use these scents to trigger sweetness and tranquility in times of need. If a person were in a stressful situation or experiencing a painful moment, they could use some lavender- or chamomile-scented oil or incense to snap themselves into a different mind frame. This technique has been used for many years as a way of bringing up dormant memories and emotions during therapy. Its application to Ayurveda, meditation, and holistic well-being is exciting and is expanding in practice. If one can use the sensual context of one's outer world to affect one's inner states of mind, the garden is a perfect place for exploring. Not only does this place one in greater connection to one's produce, but it also gives a different level of meaning to the growing process.

MEDITATIVE EXERCISE FOR THE GARDEN

Next time you have some time in the garden, stop, touch a plant, close your eyes, and breathe for a few moments. It doesn't have to be a long activity—for a short period, really focus on the feeling of a leaf or flower. Breathe three or four deep belly breaths. Feel your inner space and notice any changes or movement in energy or sensation. Smell the plant. Open your eyes periodically to admire its beauty and intelligently designed structure. Be as present as possible, maybe even more than you ever have been before with a plant.

If it seems weird at first, good! Let it be weird! Feel the presence and energy of this living being, just as you would if you were experiencing this closeness with another person or with an animal. Breathe deeply with it, visualizing the circulation of inner and outer air exchange. Experience it fully with gratitude and respect, understanding that shortly, this plant or its produce will literally be a part of you—your personal body, impacting your emotions and thoughts, providing your life with sustenance. Acknowledge that you are outwardly experiencing a small, predigested piece of yourself. See the simple truth of this strange concept. This living, thriving, bountiful piece of life will be a part of you. Its taste will affect you, its condition will impact your eating experience, its qualities will alter yours, and its content will nourish your own. Some of this plant will literally become building material for your cells. Feel it, smell it, appreciate it. Silently say, "Thank you," and sit with this reflection on your heart.

Spend five to ten minutes in silence with this understanding. Let the mind roam as it wants, paying little attention to its content. Rather, focus on the experience and presence of the plant or plants around you. Breathe deeply throughout the whole experience, giving and receiving prana in the form of shared space and air.[54] When the time is up, simply sit, and do not be too quick to jump back into activity. Let any thoughts, sensations, or emotions wash over you and settle back into the moment. If you are doing this while in the garden, it would be a great mental space to work from, as your actions will naturally be careful, gentle, nurturing, and mindful of your plants.

---

54 The definition of prana is the universal energy that flows in currents in and around the body; sometimes known as breath, considered a life-giving force. Prana will be discussed further in chapter 9.

CHAPTER 6

BRINGING THE SPIRIT

CHANTING, CHIMING, GROUNDING, AND AMBIENCE

"He who knows what sweets and virtues are in the ground, the waters, the plants, the heavens, and how to come at these enchantments, is the rich and royal man."

—*Ralph Waldo Emerson*

Do you remember a time in your life when you believed in magic? Not the "magic" of fantasy, but the genuine belief in unseen forces and the manipulation of those energies. Depending on your spiritual beliefs, magic and miracles may still be a part of how you see the world. Unfortunately, most adults lose this side of themselves as they grow up. Unless one practices a modern belief system based on nature magic—Wicca, paganism, voodoo, and so on—the notion of spiritual manipulation through nature is probably a foreign concept. However, for some, spirituality and nature are organically intertwined. You may feel the deepest sense of peace when outside in your garden. As discussed in the previous chapter, there are many reasons for this, both physical and spiritual. So far, most of the focus has been on the effects that nature can have on you, but now let's talk about what you can bring to the situation to help yourself and your garden thrive.

We started this chapter thinking about magic, witches, and wizards because so much of their activity, even in fairy tales, is based on nature. Rituals were and still are traditionally performed outdoors, if not in the wild. Many magical ceremonies and cultural events still incorporate some natural elements, ranging from gems and stones to special woods or herbs, and even animal bones or feathers. They all may hold their own specific significance, but the overall reason for this inclusion is to bring some of nature into the affair.

While you may have never considered gardening as having any connection to these kinds of practices, there may be more synergy here than you know. One of America's top farming publications, *The Farmer's Almanac*, is just an example of how these two worlds coalesce. To this day, you will see predictions and recommendations made in this, and similar publications, that are very much based on old, "witchy" science. Observing the moon cycles and weather patterns, taking into account systematic activity in the environment, and using this data to determine how one gardens or farms is, quintessentially, what being in tune with the power of nature is all about.

Framed in a different light and watered down, such publications merely provide the public with the same information one may have had to go to a shaman for centuries ago. Specialized advice like "best days for" categories for various activities is essentially the same as getting a witch to divine the best course of action. Nature speaks to us all, all the time, but only those who are in tune with it actually hear what is being said. This is, indeed, a skill, and there are those who dedicate their lives and enormous amounts of time to acquire these realizations. It is not necessary for every individual to know the natural world to this degree. However, the ability to commune with nature in these ways is extremely valuable, and accessible for anyone. The garden can be an opening to gaining this kind of wisdom for yourself.

There is a shared connection between all those who turn to nature for understanding. This connection crosses all cultural and religious boundaries. Ultimately, it is based on how one sees the natural world. To receive spiritual power or understanding from nature, one must first *be* spiritual in nature. This can come about from a range of activities, whether it be prayer, meditation, ritual, chanting, or dance. Regardless, it is the spirit that one brings into nature that determines how nature deals with you.

To ancient peoples of the world, every aspect of nature was divine and worthy of attention. Some cultures even went so far as to assign gods, goddesses, spirits, angels, nymphs, and so on to virtually everything in the forests and waterways around them. To the point, in Kemet (the ancient kingdom of Egypt/Nubia), the name given to God Almighty, Creator, Progenitor, and Source of All Things, is Neter—from which we get the very word *nature*! The other, perhaps more familiar gods were known as the Neteru, to further cement the connection.

As we have discussed, this kind of cosmological conception of the divine within the physical natural world could be found all over the world at different stages of human development. People instinctively knew that the world, and they, originated from a source, which therefore was present and accessible in everything. Another great example of this truth is found in the Celtic culture of ancient Europe. The people of this culture were famously in tune with nature and often connected with the spiritual realm through the elements. As ancient Roman author Claudius Aelianus recounts from the testimony of Euxodus in *On the Nature of Animals*, speaking of the Galatians (a group of Celts), "When locusts invade their country in clouds and damage the crops, they put up certain prayers and offer sacrifices warranted to charm birds. And the birds lend an ear and come in a united host and destroy the locusts."[55]

---

55 Claudius Aelianus, *Aelian: On the Nature of Animals, Book 7*, translated by A. F. Scholfield (Cambridge: Harvard Universtiy Press, 1951).

While one can neither confirm nor deny such claims today, these reports were common in the ancient world. Native Americans also are renowned to this day as having a very deep spiritual connection to the planet. This attitude, even if only residually, had to affect the way these people experienced nature. This level of respect and appreciation may have been the reason early medicine people and shamans were able to gain so much medicinal information from the plant world. Maybe by turning to nature with gratitude and awareness, these people could intuit the blessings before them and live in harmony with their environment.

Certainly, one's intention and energy can go a long way in determining one's experience of nature. We can see this even in the most mundane ways. For instance, when engaging in normal outdoor activities such as hiking, one may notice a difference between having a peaceful, settled energy that is comfortable and being anxious, on guard, fearful, or distrusting of the environment. The feeling of hiking with someone who is afraid of every little tickle or noise in nature versus one who is completely at ease, explorative, and blissed out is definitely noticeable.

This is due to the energy of the individual, not to any difference in the setting. One person can spend hours in the garden exploring, observing, and fixing, while another may grow bothered and tired of the whole thing within a few minutes. It is all about perspective and personal energy. With that said, for us to cultivate a spiritual relationship with our gardens, we must bring a little bit of our spirits into the matter. We must first deal with our personal energy, and then use it to affect the garden with a little bit of our spiritual presence.

Through Ayurveda and similar holistic systems, we are taught to treat every piece of life as a significant aspect of the whole. Also, these disciplines emphasize the use of the natural elements for self-healing. When gardening, we must cultivate a different mind-set than the traditional one of seeing the garden as just a food source. It is an opportunity to heal and be healed, to nourish and be nourished, a relationship and connection between yourself and your food. Treating the plants as living creatures, using the garden as a spiritual space, and approaching it all with respect and reverence, one can come to realize far more magic in one's gardens than one may have ever thought possible.

SETTING THE SCENE

The ways in which we plot and decorate our gardens can have greater significance when intentionally cultivating a spiritual space. From grand designs, mazes, and ornamented walkways to simply placing some spiritually themed statues around the area, these visuals can serve as reminders of the presence of the divine in your garden. Some even go so far as to create altars, prayer spaces, or display symbols in or around the garden to accomplish this. Whatever does it for you, give it a try! The goal is to create a spiritual atmosphere out in this natural setting. Tibetan prayer flags and tapestries are another excellent option for enhancing the visuals of your garden. If you decide to grow flowering plants with beautiful colors and foliage, you may want to keep your artificial decorations to a minimum, as nature will definitely outshine anything you could possibly do to your garden. However, these kinds of enhancements can be a nice touch.

Consider the main objectives of your garden, as this will play a role in choosing your best design. For instance, a kitchen-garden design will be more intricate due to its need to serve multiple purposes, so you may section off areas for herbs or other specified groups. You may also design your garden with emphasis on the visual pleasure it will provide in bloom; therefore, placement of flowers and other landscape features will weigh heavier with you. Decide what effects will influence you the most spiritually or emotionally, and choose your garden based on that. Here's an example of how to approach this part of the process:

KNOW WHAT YOU WANT

I like having the sitting area of the garden near the aromatic plants. I find the smells to be enjoyable during meditation, as every breeze gives the senses a new delight. I also find myself relaxed by the wind and air qualities of being outside. I love the expanse of nature and find panoramic views to be inspiring. I'd like an area to entertain as well as be by myself and enjoy the sights and sounds of the garden. Also, I find birds and butterflies beautiful.

SPIRITUAL GARDENING
APPROACH TO DESIGN

There are several things to unpack in this example that will become more identifiable as you learn. First, in this example, I am very much a wind person. This corresponds with space and air elements within nature. To bring the relaxation of these elements into my garden, I would place any statues, altars, or similar pieces in an area where I can get a full view. This means that sitting areas for prayer and meditation or socializing would better serve me if they were on either end of the garden or beside it, as opposed to being among the plants. I would plant all my flowers and fragrant herbs near that end of the garden.

To enhance the effects of the wind, I would place wind chimes and similar ornaments near the seating area. I may also want to add some tapestries scattered in the garden to blow in the wind and keep a spiritual theme present. This kind of logic would best serve in setting a proper garden scene. If you are more water based, place your fountains and baths near the sitting area. Maybe incorporate a koi pond in the center of your garden. Plot your garden according to the things about nature that you find pleasurable or meditative.

The sight and sound of water has been known to put human beings into transcendent inner experiences. Sometimes, this can happen passively, as when strolling along a river or creek. Water creates an atmosphere of peace. It is this kind of attention to the atmosphere of your garden that we are focusing on. It helps to think of the result when planning your garden. How do you want to feel while there? Will you be spending time relaxing in or near the garden, and where is it best suited to do so? Water effects like birdbaths are great because they act as a way of inviting nature into your presence and can even serve to deter birds from your produce when placed with that in mind. If you are one who enjoys birds, a birdbath can add some real excitement to your time outdoors. Even while one is gardening, one can enjoy the sound and sight of these special creatures.

Similarly, koi ponds and frog ponds can intensify your garden experience. During moments of reflection and silence, a pond or fountain can be especially serene and place you in a more meditative mode. This, once again, draws from the natural spiritual power of the water element. Additionally, one is doing some karmic good by providing these spaces for the creatures around your property to drink and congregate. From a certain perspective, it can be seen as an all-around act of goodwill and intention, making the space more enjoyable and encouraging longer time spent in the garden.

In this same spirit, specialized pathways, mazes, overhangs, and trellises are good for inspiring longer time in the garden. Aside from merely giving you more to look at, these too can be spiritually themed. Mazes are great for this. Buddhist and other monastic traditions are fond of this kind of garden design, citing that it encourages mindfulness and long, peaceful walks, and stills one's thoughts. The thought of creating a maze for your garden may sound outlandish, but one can easily create small versions using stones and edgers that would be appropriate for your garden space. Doing so, keep in mind that it is not so much about creating a true maze as it is about having a walkway that attracts visitors as a cool visual and gives the mind something to focus on while one is passively enjoying the surroundings.

If you decide to build this kind of structure, be aware that even the construction of it can be meditative, and you should put some consideration into every aspect of its design for the walkway to be effective in this way. Here is an example of how one would approach building a meditative maze for a small garden area:

1. Decide on the area and size you would like to dedicate to the maze. Also, consider what kind of maze you would like to have. Will this be a simple footpath that meanders through the plants in your garden? If you have the space, you may even consider a walled maze, using shrubbery, raised beds, trees, crop rows, fencing, and so on to create a defined path.

For a moderate garden size, I recommend the footpath. These are easy to do and do not necessarily require much in materials. You can create this kind of pathway using small rock, pebbles, pavers, wood, or any other material you can think of. Another benefit of this style is that it can easily be changed or removed by picking up the material. When one incorporates the plants themselves into the path via raised beds or in-ground planting, change becomes more of a hassle for the gardener and the plant life. If you want to make your path out of trees or shrubs, be sure of your design before planting. Also, raised beds can be heavy once they have been filled and plants take root.

If your garden will be in a secure area, you can add some spiritual energy by placing gems, crystals, geodes, and so on along the path. This is highly recommended, especially if you will have areas of the garden centered for meditation sitting spaces, altars, benches, and the like. Remember to have fun and give all your creativity to it, and keep in mind that you are making a space you plan to spend a lot of time in, both in work and reflection.

2. Pick a design pattern for your pathway. Will this be a true maze, or just a wandering walkway? Do you want it to be incorporated into the garden—that is, weaving between your crop rows, centered among the plants, and so on? Or would you prefer to have your path near a sectioned-off garden, leading you around certain areas or plant rows? If you do not know and just want to try it out, it may help to browse templates for maze designs online or find one through other research. Depending on your spiritual practice, the actual path can be another form of expression. Designs can create crosses, fish, stars, mandalas, or whatever you would prefer. Just draw it out.

3. Bring your drawing or template out to your garden site and survey where you would be building this. What obstructions might there be—tree roots, large stones, buildings? Are there hills or other features of the terrain? You may be able to incorporate these into your path, but if they have not already been considered, this is the time to plan around any that you see. It may also spark some other ideas to be there. Walk the area and imagine what your walkway will look like and how it will flow with your garden and other landscaping. While doing this, consider views that hold any significance, plants that you want to pass next to, and areas that need to be a part of it.

4. Lay the path. If you will be planting to create boundaries, just mark off where you would like people to walk. Line your path with whatever materials you have chosen. Something to consider here is how you would like to maintain the path. Will this space be large enough to require routine mowing or trimming? Some opt for the use of stone pavers as an easy and reversible option. Gravel and pebblestone can also be used, but this is usually costly, and some small stones will likely end up among your plants. Also, weeds will undoubtedly pop up between the stones, so you may want to lay black tarp or some other means of control beforehand. For a simpler process, setting pieces of wood, bricks, stone, or pavers is sufficient.

5. Accentuate. Once you have laid the path of your walk, think of what you would like to see. This would be the time to place any statues, birdbaths, fountains, tapestry, or trellises in their spots. Consider which plants you will grow in various areas. How will they grow as they mature—will they vine, branch widely, or cover the ground? Take all this into account. For instance, the vining growth of cucumbers can be combined with a decorative trellis. Or the tall growth of sunflowers or corn could add obstruction and boundary to a

pathway. Elephant ears may add good shade for your meditation area or pond. Vibrantly colored flowers may be bunched together for a beautiful scene around a spiritually significant figurine. If you take the time to know your plants and apply some imagination, you may be surprised at some of the extravagance that can be created right at home.

Sound makers can also add to your gardening experience. As previously mentioned, energy is a big factor in how one meets nature and how the garden will respond to your input. Energy is vibratory in nature, and humanity has long known of the power of sound in shifting energy. If you are connected to the air and space elements, you may find the sound of wind to be calming.

If this sounds like you, including chimes and other decorations that react to the wind with sound effects may be a great addition. This will prove pleasant and give you an effortless sense of peace while in the garden. Also, it is recommended that one use as much natural material in one's decorating as possible. This has aesthetic and energetic significance. Bamboo, for example, is an excellent and sustainable option for these kinds of designs. Just remember that the goal should not be to distract from the harmonious sounds of nature. The idea is to seamlessly blend and create tranquility with every one of these enrichments.

If you want to add an extra touch of environmentalism to your gardening, create your own chimes by recycling items like glass bottles and jars, cans, pieces of wood, or other materials. This can easily be done with a little creativity and design research. By suspending these items and placing them in areas that will catch wind, you can add a simple yet impactful delight to any garden. An easy-to-build chime set might involve using sticks and fishing line to suspend a few glass bottles, then adding anything from screws to pieces of wood to enable sound.

Each of these suggestions merely adds peripheral value to the activity of the garden. For us to really bring some spiritual energy, it will require direct action.

⋙ PRAYER, CHANTING, AND TUNING ⋘

One's voice can be an important part of one's communication. Even though a significant amount of human communication is nonverbal, the power of the word has been spoken of since ancient times. As the Bible says, "A gentle tongue is a Tree of Life, but perverseness in it breaks the Spirit."[56] Or, as Buddha once said, "Speak only when you feel that your words are better than your silence." Examples of this kind of wisdom about one's speech can be found in many traditions. All of them serve the purpose of reminding you how powerful your voice can really be. Whether the subject is life manifestations, or social interactions, prayers, or just self-talk, what one says carries power. The beauty of acknowledging this is that we can harness that power and use it for our benefit.

It has been scientifically proven that plants respond to sound. For example, in an article published in the *Journal of Integrative Agriculture*, "Advances in Effects of Sound Waves on Plants," scientists concluded that "using sound waves for desirable plants could stimulate them to grow while undesirable plants (weeds for instance) could be inhibited, which has been done with

---

56 Biblica, Prov. 15:4.

electromagnetic energy, in this case sound waves, pulsed to the right set of frequencies thus affecting the plant at an energetic and submolecular level."[57] The scientific research on this plant behavior is still ongoing, but the wisdom traditions of the world have always acknowledged this truth. In hopes of creating a spirit-centered garden, one can use the combined power of the human voice and plant reactivity to sound to support the growth process.

Chanting is particularly useful because it creates a trancelike state of being. This can be done using words with meaning or even just sounds as a mantra. *Mantra* is an Eastern term for words or sounds used to bring a person to a state of meditative concentration. Mantras have been used since antiquity and across many faiths. Primordial sound meditation, a technique developed and taught through the work of Deepak Chopra and the Chopra Center, is especially effective at accomplishing this state because it is based on natural sounds found in the universe. Whereas a traditional Hindu or Buddhist mantra may be a string of sayings or scripture, primordial sound meditation is composed of sounds without any direct meaning. This makes the chanting or silent repetition of the mantra take on a vibrational significance, rather than a verbal or mental one. It is this technique that is recommended here, since our goal is attunement with the natural energies that these sounds originate from.

The best and probably most familiar primordial sound is the universal sound "*aum*" (or "*om*"). You may recall using this sound as the vibrational basis of a previous meditation exercise. In fact, most Vedic traditions hold this sound to be the *pranava*, the source sound of the created universe. It is believed that the Big Bang, which gave birth to everything in existence, was the utterance of this sound, and that all of this is still rooted in "*aum*." It is highly revered and used across many faiths and disciplines, including Yoga, Vedanta, Jainism, Buddhism, Hinduism, and Zoroastrianism.

---

57 H. E. Hassanien Reda et al., "Advances in Effects of Sound Waves on Plants," *Journal of Integrative Agriculture* 13, no. 2 (2013): 335–348.

The power of this sound is proven, as it has a place in many other languages across the world and almost always has some spiritual context. To this day, members of all Abrahamic faiths use the word *amen* to close prayers or affirm truth. *Amen* is even linguistically derived from the sound "*aum.*" In ancient Kemet (Egypt), several chief deities were given names that were concealments or alterations of the sound, including Amun, Aten, Ra, Ausar (Osiris), and Auset (Isis). The presumed intention behind this was to convey the powerful connection with the source of life and with the supremacy assigned to these beings.

The presence of this sound is felt across a wide spectrum. Within the primordial-sound technique, one's concentration is fixed on repeating this one sound as one slips into a receptive, meditative state of being. In some cases, the sound may be flanked by other sounds, but there still would not be a specific meaning applied to the mantra. The real power of this technique, for our purposes, can be found in chanting it aloud.

Since "*aum*" connects all of life, it is highly effective in connecting a gardener and plants. Chanting "*aum*" while working in the garden has demonstrated testable effects such as increased growth, optimal health and beauty of the plants, and fuller produce. One can chant other sounds or sing pleasant songs and get good results as well. The intention of the person and the energy presented seem to be the only factors that profoundly affect the plant. It is recommended here, however, that one starts out by chanting "*aum*," because it is simple and universal. But feel free to play with it however you choose. If singing praises to Jesus in the garden does it for you, then by all means do so. Similarly, if repeating your favorite prayers or songs brings about a pleasant mood in you, these will also be fine. Remember that this principle works based on vibration, energy, intention, and frequency.

In line with this is the practice of chakra tuning, which has been promoted in the West through Yoga. A lot can be said about chakras. In short, *chakra* is a Sanskrit term pertaining to energetic focal points within the body where the spiritual and physical forces within a human being meet. This knowledge, and the manipulation of these energy centers, are attributed to the science of tantra, but because of their common scriptural origins and culture, you will find quite a bit about chakras in Yogic philosophy.

This wisdom, like much of the other information we have explored so far, can be seen in other spiritual disciplines as well. Notably, traditional Chinese medicine also developed healing techniques that deal with this concept. Methods that have survived throughout the ages, such as the use of acupuncture and certain massage-therapy procedures, are based on this same understanding of the holistic human system. However, it is in ancient India that we find it most widely used and investigated.

Like the doshas, chakras can become unstable, imbalanced, or weakened by one's life experiences, diet, and habits. Therefore, one of the healing therapies that developed is the use of primordial sounds that correspond to certain areas of the body and that, when chanted or heard, appear to tune the chakras back into balance. Scientific research on the efficacy of this method is scarce; however, millions of practitioners spanning centuries attest to its power. One can test this through direct experience and should do so frequently. Simply by saying these sounds out loud, you will feel inner vibration that generally corresponds to the areas it is prescribed to.

The fact that these sounds hold significance in nature or in the inner spiritual dimensions is only a testament to the inner connectivity of the universe and how tuned in these people must have been to intuit such knowledge. While there is much to unpack about chakras, the main relevance of the subject to this work comes in performing this chakra tuning alongside the plants in your garden. If chanting a singular primordial sound can have benefits for the person and the garden, routinely performing a full body tune-up can only add value.

The primordial sounds used in chakra tuning are as follows:

- **Crown**—enlightenment, spiritual realization, evolution, and so on (top of the head): "*aum*"
- **Third eye**—insight, intuition (middle of the head, between the eyes): "*sham*"
- **Throat**—expression, personal truth (from the middle of the neck to the collarbone): "*ham*"
- **Heart**—love, joy, connection (middle of the chest): "*yam*"
- **Solar plexus**—personal will, drive, desire (the stomach/gut/torso area): "*ram*"
- **Sacral**—creativity, sexual energy, enjoyment (the pelvic region, below the belly button): "*vam*"
- **Root**—support, sustainability, survival (the tailbone, the bottom of the spine): "*lam*"

Each sound is spoken with an extended "*aahhhhmm*" sound at the end and should be extended as much as possible without strain when performing a tuning. To perform this properly, one starts at the root sound of "*lam*" and works one's way up the spine to "*aum*." Styles of doing this may differ, with some speaking the sound only one time each and some repeating each sound for a prescribed amount of time (i.e., seven times each); others may even go up and then come back down the spine. Depending on what discipline you are referencing, there are reasons and situations for any version you would choose.

However, the consensus and only staple is to start at the root and move up to the crown, or descend from the crown to the root—always in order. Also, one should close this practice by chanting "*aum*," as is customary with this kind of inner work. Some even choose to specialize the pranava at the end by extending and exaggerating the sound to more of an "*aaaaahhhh-uuuuuuu-mmmmm*" sound, with each part of the "word" singled out, as opposed to "*om*." It is recommended too that one do this whenever one feels the need to energize the body, or when one has issues in the areas of life that correspond to the specific chakra centers. These can be chanted individually for specific reasons but are most powerful when sounded out together in the manner described.

Doing this in your garden is helpful, as it not only provides you with personal benefits but also reverberates in your surroundings as the sound carries. If you feel uncomfortable about doing this in earshot of others or have a small location for your garden and nearby neighbors, it can be performed softly and quietly too. The more the sound is projected, however, the more effective it is generally thought to be. But doing it at all, even inwardly and silently, has its merits. Your plants will thank you in their own way for this time spent with them and for the vibrations you are sharing.

⋙⋙ GROUNDING ⋘⋘

As with *chakras*, you may be familiar with this term through Yoga. Grounding, sometimes called Earthing, is the process of realigning your body's electrical system by close contact with that of the Earth. As in grounding a mechanical electric current, the ions in our bodies are renewed and recalibrated through this therapy. This is reported to have many benefits for the body and mind. The most intriguing of these for the medical community have been findings of immune support, positive effects on blood clarity and cardiovascular health, and relief of chronic pain. Much more research must be done before the masses will be convinced, however. The beauty of grounding/Earthing is that one can try it for oneself and prove its value. From a physical science perspective, the concept is logical. We know that the body generates electrical energy, and we know that grounding aligns with how electricity generally works.

There are a few methods for Earthing, but they all involve getting close to the soil. The most common way is to go barefoot in the dirt. This works perfectly with gardening, as some find the sensation of moist, nutrient-rich soil on their bare feet to be soothing. One can easily do a little bit of grounding while inspecting one's plants or performing other duties around the garden. Since these tasks must be done regularly, it offers the gardener plenty of opportunity to test it out.

Another grounding method is to lie flat on the ground for a period. Although some prefer this way of doing it, standing upright or walking seems to be more aligned with the science behind the practice. Since the body's electrical energy primarily travels vertically with the spine, it seems logical that this would be the most effective. Also, grounding while standing is easier to pair with other activities. However, it is suggested that you try both techniques to find your best fit and comfortability. For an added benefit, try chanting the sound "*lam*" while grounding. Since this chakra sound corresponds to the root chakra, the tuning of its energy can be complementary to the goals of Earthing.

Each of the techniques suggested in this chapter is meant to help create the atmosphere for spiritual energy to flow between the gardener and his or her garden. Whether one focuses on the aesthetics of the garden or on aligning one's personal energy, all must be in cooperation with the general purpose of accessing the spiritual dimensions of the hobby. By following these exercises and giving awareness to the main intention of spiritual connection, soon you will feel the effects on the garden space and find it peacefully opening its spiritual energy to receive and nourish your own.

CHAPTER 7

DOING THE WORK

"Gardens are not made by singing, 'Oh, how beautiful!'
and sitting in the shade."

—*Rudyard Kipling*

If you are already accustomed to gardening, you know it requires a good deal of time and attention to maintain. Some spend enormous amounts of time and energy creating their botanical paradise, while others just do enough to keep it from getting taken over by weeds.

Skillful gardening is an art form. There is a reason professional gardeners and landscaping companies exist and that not every farm produces as well as others. There is a special touch, a true green thumb, some humans are gifted with. But what if this so-called green thumb was nothing more than a genuine love of plant life and their care—an instinctual connection, rooted in love and enjoyment of the outdoors, elements, nature, and so on? That is not to even speak of tilling, weeding, pruning, picking, harvesting, and so on. Although these activities are leisurely most of the time, the condition of the environment can make them a little bit of a workout and a chore.

Whether one is out in the hot sun during summer, working in wet, muddy conditions, or just dealing with a fresh crop of sprouting weeds after every spring rain, gardening is not always comfortable. In fact, many of the best-producing crops and most magnificent botanical gardens were created as hard-fought, sometimes inconvenient, and often sweaty labors of love. As the Bible famously records in the exile of Adam and Eve from the Garden of Eden:

All the days of your life.
Both thorns and thistles it shall grow for you;
And you will eat the plants of the field;
By the sweat of your face
You will eat bread . . .[58]

Your mental approach is everything when it comes to working in a garden. If you are one who enjoys being outside or even in a greenhouse, taking in the freshness, the colors and smells of plants, observing the growth and changes, and so on, working will feel like true collaboration with the Earth. Gardeners who love these elements will see weeding as beautifying or accenting the plants. They will look at tending the soil and daily watering as time well spent, an act of nourishing love toward the plant, not a chore. Gardeners will protect the plants from pests and weather damage. They will do everything for the well-being of the plant with genuine interest rather than thinking only of production. Gardeners in love with the craft delight in the progress of the plants and the produce.

This is the attitude that must be cultivated. Love is the key factor in whether you will enjoy your garden. The intention here is not so much to focus on the obvious beauty and productivity these positive emotions engender in the plants, but to see the effects they have on the gardener as well.

---

[58] Biblica, Gen. 3:17–19.

The discipline and dedication to produce your best garden can permeate other areas of your life. Take goal manifestation or realization, for instance. By now, certain practices like vision boarding and mindful affirmations are fairly mainstream as means to accomplish goals. They were once thought to be a little fantastical, but now, more people are accepting the idea that our thoughts shape our realities. In line with this logic, they are encouraged to tend the gardens of their minds—to be aware of persistent thoughts, emotions, and habits, as well as their impact on life.

Similarly, in gardening, one must stay on task, because nature is in full support of not only one's desirable plants but also all other forms of life within the space. Invasive species, weeds, vines, and creatures of all kinds are constantly working to unravel your perfect vision for your garden. This is more than a metaphoric comparison, and both take their own kind of work and consistency. The use of a vision board is meant to routinely bring one's awareness to one's desires and goals—in effect, training one to grow one's life in a certain direction. A garden provides a similar service to the practitioner, in that it can routinely bring a sense of peace, simplicity, and space to one's daily routine. As these qualities are worthy of cultivation, one can envision the garden in this way and transform a chore into a blessing—as, in a sense, another form of meditation, even while one is active. It's all about intention and perception.

What goes into a successful garden? What preparation is required for the space? How much of the actual growth process is the responsibility of the gardener, and how much is left to the whims of nature? What does a gardener actually do?

This chapter will provide some of the basics of gardening work and the factors one must consider:

1. Minding the soil
2. Seed sowing
3. Watering
4. Weeding and pruning
5. Harvesting

»»»» MINDING THE SOIL «««

This factor of gardening is often overlooked despite being one of the most important aspects of growing. Some go so far as to test the chemistry of the soil routinely and manipulate its composition. While this is a great tool for maximizing growth and produce, it is not always necessary to get very technical about it. If you live in an area that generally produces good vegetative growth in the wild, most likely your vegetables, fruits, herbs, and so on will thrive as well. However, if you are seeking to grow specific plants, especially exotic varieties, or you live in an area that does not naturally support those plants, you may want to dig a little deeper into this part of the process. Making sure your soil is as nutritive and fertile as possible is the goal.

The three factors that one must consider when it comes to soil are pH, nutritive content, and soil type. Some plants require a certain chemistry in order to thrive. These characteristics are usually listed when purchasing soil or can be ascertained from simple observation. pH can easily be tested using one of several commercial products available on the market. These will come in either digital testers or paper strip tests. Based on the results of your test, you can adjust the acidity of your soil by adding products, such as lime, which is great for increasing pH, or adding organic matter to lessen it.

According to the latest assessments of *The Old Farmer's Almanac,* the ideal pH for most vegetable gardens is 6.0–7.0 on a pH scale ranging from 0 to 14—so, fairly neutral. This range is said to be ideal for root growth and microbial activity.[59] Every plant is different, however, so definitely do some research into which range is best. You may still be able to get some growth while skipping this step, but if you want ideal results, be mindful of this.

---

59 "Soil Preparation: How Do You Prepare Garden Soil for Planting?" The Old Farmer's Almanac, March 5, 2021, https://www.almanac.com/preparing-soil-planting.

Nutritive content of the soil is normally in reference to the amount of organic material present. Manure, compost, and fertilizers are the most common additives. The key chemicals to consider in your soil's nutrition are generally nitrogen, phosphorus, and potassium. If you are purchasing commercial soil, the details of the soil composition should be listed on the packaging and should list these elements. However, calcium, magnesium, zinc, and iron are just a few of the other important elements that should also be present in the soil. An easy way to analyze this is to look at your daily supplements or recommended mineral intake. The sad truth is that a significant amount of the naturally sourced minerals we used to get from our foods has been depleted due to commercial farming practices. As Ronald Amundson, a professor of environmental science, policy, and management at the University of California, Berkeley, has stated, "Ever since humans developed agriculture, we've been transforming the planet and throwing the soil's nutrient cycle out of balance."[60]

SEED SOWING

Choosing which seeds to sow in the ground is obviously vital to the gardening process. Part of the fun is picking through seeds and imagining what they'll end up like. In a childlike way, this part of the experience is more about fun, imagination, and experimentation. Intuition can also play a role in this action, as one is literally handpicking the fate of a plant to live and produce more life.

Not that it needs to be taken too seriously, but seed selection should be done with awareness. In a commercial farming operation, seed source and potency are of the utmost importance. More than likely, you are not staking your livelihood on your crops, but you may want to be mindful of your seed choices for the same reasons. First of all, there is the actual plotting of the garden. What plants and produce

---

60 Lucy Draper, "Risk of Fertiliser Cartels Controlling World's Food Supply by 2050, Says Study," Newsweek, May 7, 2015, https://www.newsweek.com/ risk-fertiliser-cartels-controlling-worlds-food-supply-by-2050-says-study-326994.

are you most interested in growing? What will be of use to you and your family? What do you just want to have around for fragrance, beauty, and ambience? How do each of these types of plants grow? Do they require more or less space?

These are the kinds of questions to keep in mind when choosing. Do the research and know your seeds. Remember that these are living creatures with their own character and needs. Some like more sun than others. Some seeds need to be planted deep, while others are just scattered across the surface of the ground and watered. Knowing these key factors and treating the seeds accordingly can make a world of difference in what you get out of your garden. For instance, cucumber, pepper, and tomato seeds require minimal burying, preferring to be just beneath the surface. Some peppers can literally just be sprinkled along the ground and produce results, making them pretty easy. Be mindful of the sowing needs of your plants. This is just the beginning of your role in the creative process. Start here with the cultivation of this attitude. You are not just throwing some seeds out and seeing what happens. This is a deliberate act.

Aside from the food or medicine that you will receive from this plant, you are part of the natural selection process of this species. Just as one lucky sperm made it to your mother's egg and solidified your birth, so do you choose one among these plants to continue life. These seeds will root, grow, develop, flower, re-create, and die as every other living creature does, including yourself. So even though it may not be a matter of life and death to you, your role in the potential life of this plant is vital at this moment. Act consciously, and you will see that it opens the door for greater connection and appreciation of the plants in your garden.

WATERING

As we all know, water is essential to life on this planet. Access to water is one of the primary drives in every creature. For plants to function properly, they must be watered properly and regularly according to their individual needs.

As a gardener, providing nourishment for your plants will be your primary responsibility, and watering is a huge part of the job. The most important factors to remember are water quality, regularity, and being mindful of the soil. Does your soil drain well, or does it hold water? Is it rocky, or clumpy, or does it contain a lot of clay? These can affect how well the plant's roots are able to absorb the water and how it will grow.

If you are sowing directly into the soil on your property, you will have to manipulate this by tilling and sprinkling gardening soil into that which is found around your home. Testing the soil with a kit can help if you are in doubt about the ability of the ground to nourish a garden. Use a shovel to break up your dirt, and test its value as gardening soil. Some areas have soil with a high clay content, and this is not always suited to gardening. Vegetables especially have a hard time with high clay content, making it more difficult for them to take root.

Once you have broken up the soil, add an appropriate amount of nutrient-rich gardening soil to the plot and then till it in or rake the dirt together to mix on the surface and give your plants a helping hand. You may even consider an entire layer of dark, loose gardening soil in those circumstances. Avoiding this process is one of the advantages of raised beds, in which the gardener can even differentiate the soil in various beds. If you decide to incorporate trees like firs, birches, and maples, note that they prefer rocky, gravelly soil, as do aloe plants and many flowering herbs. The importance of this aspect of a garden is in its effect on water retention. Compact soils, like those containing clay, are not easily penetrated, creating problems for most garden plants. Soil that is too porous can drain off at a speed that is not ideal for a plant that requires a lot of water to fruit. These are all reasons for the gardener to do diligent research into ideal conditions for what they are growing.

When watering, keep in mind which plants can have more water and which require less. Some plants are extremely sensitive to flooding or overwatering, barely requiring water to grow. Others like a lot of water. As a rule, you do not have to worry about your in-ground plants suffering from overwatering. Apart from times of flooding, and growing plants like watermelon that produce low-lying fruit, water is not the issue. The soil is pretty resourceful at dispersing the excess water when given enough time.

If you plot your garden with all your desired plants and their characteristics considered, this should not be difficult. Perhaps you can place all the plants that will require a lot of water in the same few rows or area of the garden. This way, one avoids damaging less thirsty plants. For example, certain herbs, like basil and parsley, require a lot more water than their counterparts. You would not want them growing right next to rosemary, sage, oregano, thyme, lavender, or most mints, because these may die from overwatering. Cucumbers and melons require way more water than peppers. Simply put, know your plants.

However, these considerations are basic to a garden. Evolution takes place once you can nourish your garden with love and consciousness. To a plant, water is everything. While it may draw nutrients from the soil and energy from the sun, all of it works because of the presence of water. As a gardener, you are taking on the responsibility for virtually everything your plants are able to do.

Nature will do all the real work, but with your assistance, the plants will thrive rather than merely survive. In most parts of the world, it does not rain every day during the growing season. Tropical environments may be more supportive in this way, but in many cases, your plants will receive natural rain only periodically. For some, this may be plenty, but a lot of the plants we use as food and medicine will require routine watering, so how and when you water your garden is key.

If your goal is to turn this time into a fuller meditative experience, shortly after sunrise or at sunset works well. These are typically times when the energy is right for meditation and can be used for this purpose as well. You may say to yourself, "But I'm just holding a water hose or operating a sprinkler. What is spiritual about that?" This is a valid question. However, it is only a matter of perspective.

In truth, everything we do can be seen from the spiritual dimension. All that is required is a little awareness and understanding of the underlying principles of the activity. Watering your garden is, all at once, an act of nourishment and a pastime, in the sense that you are required to spend anywhere from five to fifteen minutes of your day engaged with your garden. Even in the backyard, greenhouse, porch, or growing room, this counts as time with nature. Unfortunately, many of us are cut off from the natural elements in our modern-day lifestyles. Effort and time set aside for nature is the only way some people get any real exposure to it at all. However, if it is, know that simply watering your garden with the right attitude and care is an important interaction with this part of life.

While nourishing your garden, pay attention to the plants. Notice how they perk up and look livelier with a little water. This is perceptible if you have a plant that has gotten a little dry during the day. The colors become more vibrant, the leaves and flowers spread open, the stem stands a little more erect—signs that your plants are happy. Like a nutrient-deprived person after a much-needed meal and drink, your plants will visibly show that they have been satiated. Noticing this builds appreciation for your participation in this process. See with your own eyes the effect your action has on them. Receive their beauty and effervescence as a way of saying, "Thank you."

Additionally, use this activity to experience yourself as a giver. Fully take on this role with the intention of conditioning the subconscious to extend this role into other areas of life. You are the source of nourishment in your world. Your attention and awareness are the waters flowing into the growing parts of your life. Your love pours out where it is needed. You are the life-giving flow of energy, responsible for all, caring for everything.

⧸⧸⧸⧸ WEEDING AND PRUNING ⧸⧸⧸⧸

When people think of working hard in the garden, weeding and pruning are usually two of the first activities that come to mind. It is true that for most, this is not the fun part of being in the garden. It's dirty and sometimes uncomfortable, and you can get minor cuts and bruises. It's the part that requires the most attention and discipline. However, in nature's timeless wisdom, it is also the most rewarding work of the garden as well. It brings you into active engagement with a microcosmic part of the wild, untamed aspects of nature. When your job is to make straight the crooked rows, to trim back the vigorous growth, to enforce human order on nature's beautiful chaos, the work can seem never-ending and arduous. It is important when maintaining your garden that you stop to appreciate it routinely and deliberately. In fact, it is recommended to make it a ritual of sorts. Spend five to ten minutes each day during the growing season to admire your collaborative work with nature.

It may actually help in the beginning to make rituals of all aspects of your time in the garden. This can provide motivation and structure to stick to it and serve as a time to review your work for improvement. During growing season, I like to start my mornings off with reflective time in the garden. Usually, it is still moist and dewy, and slightly cool as the sun starts to rise. When my schedule allows, I find this to be a great time for meditation. Afterward, I like doing the weeding and other physical work while still in the cool of the day (from about 8:30 to 10:30 a.m.). It is a great time for this because the coolness makes it more enjoyable.

If work or school interfere, the evening is equally good for these reasons. I have always preferred to make the evening time about watering. For a beginning gardener, it may be easier to remember to water your garden in the evening, as it is normally a slowing-down period in the day and easily incorporated into one's schedule. I schedule a lot of my garden activities by the sun, avoiding the hard work when the sun is at its peak, getting in tune to jump-start my day as the sun rises, and cooling down and nourishing as the sun sets. With in-ground planting, your garden will need to be watered routinely, if not daily. When you choose potted or raised-bed gardening, you may find that some of your plants require less water. It is during the watering times that I most enjoy looking over my handiwork and the growth of the garden.

While the getting-your-hands-dirty part of gardening is routinely required, if you stay on top of it, it is not as time-consuming or as hard. In today's fast-paced society, often these time and work challenges of gardening are not very appealing, but with dedication, it does not have to be as much of a chore. On another note, if you are a person who does not typically get much physical exercise during the day, this side of gardening can be a way to get the blood flowing. Pulling weeds and tilling your soil can be especially useful in this way, as they require more effort than most garden activities. Neither activity needs to be done every day. However, when needed, one can definitely get a work-out if that is what is desired.

The point is to enjoy being physically active and getting dirty. This is good for your health in multiple ways and goes a long way toward the betterment of your produce.

HARVESTING

The harvest is the culmination of all the planning and effort you have put into your garden. It is the reward for the hard work and should be approached as such. If you have followed the tips and guidelines outlined in this book, you will have received benefits from your garden already. However, these have been mostly spiritual and psychological. Now is the time when you get to wrap your hands—and mouth— around the literal fruit of your labor!

The kind of care and awareness described so far, when applied, should produce significant results from your plants. Take pride in them. It is important that you do! Acknowledge what you have helped nature create. Although nature does not need the help, your hands have blessed these plants. Enjoy the results, and make use of as much of the plant as you can. In this way, you are honoring both the plant being and yourself. Respectfully remove the fruit, vegetables, or foliage, taking care not to intentionally harm the plant. Even if your plant is seasonal and will die soon, receiving its fruits respectfully creates harmony and connection. As you have been encouraged all along, treat them as the living beings they are.

Be sure to research the best times to harvest particular plants, as they all have preferences. Some, if harvested correctly, will continue to live and produce for you late into the season. Be mindful of the plants, rather than coming in like a thief and simply taking what you want. Do it with grace and humility. If you feel inclined, even try saying "Thank you" while doing so. While this may seem arbitrary, remember that plants do have a form of consciousness. They can react to stimuli and interact with other species of life. As discussed above, research has shown that they respond to music, energy, and who knows what else that we have not discovered. These are living beings! Considering that you are taking from them for your personal nourishment and enjoyment, the least you could say is "Thank you." If all these other displays of consciousness hold true, who is to say that they don't receive the energy of your appreciation? Even if they do not register it at all, which is unlikely, it still does your own spirit some good to practice this gratitude toward the natural world at large.

For us to best serve ourselves and our gardens while harvesting, here are a few good practices to keep in mind.

HERB CLIPPING

Unlike harvesting produce, properly gathering herbs can take a little skill. This is a time when the differences and preferences of each plant are truly relevant. In general, if one acts with a gentle heart toward the plant, one will intuitively know when one has gone too far. However, it does require some knowledge of what is best for your individual herbs. It is recommended that you research the herbs you are growing for the best methods. Some general advice:

- **Wait until the plant has abundant foliage.** Picking too soon can be damaging to the plant's growth potential.

- **Don't be greedy!** Pick no more than one-third or so of the available amount. This way, your harvest is not too taxing on the plant. Regular clipping, when done responsibly, can be healthy for the plant.

- **Herbs are usually best when harvested in the morning.** If your herbs are growing outside, catch them just after the dew has evaporated but the oils are still present to the touch. This will maximize the potency of the harvest.

- **Know what you are harvesting.** Be clear on which part of the plant you are harvesting. This can be important for multiple reasons. For starters, some plants receive more damage from specific parts. If the plant is going to continue to produce for you, you should be aware of the best practices to encourage that growth. For instance, if you are harvesting the foliage of the plant, start clipping before the flowers bloom. In almost all plants that bloom, this marks a significant moment in the plant's life, and many qualities undergo change. Taste, texture, potency, and, in some cases, even toxicity levels change after flowering. Also, clipping before blooming trains the plant to direct energy toward foliage and not flowering, which can prolong your harvest in some plants. If you are harvesting the flower part of the plant, it is best done right before the flower is fully opened. It will be at its most potent.

FRUITS AND VEGETABLES

When harvesting anything from a plant, one must practice careful consideration of the whole plant body and its functionality. In the case of fruits and vegetables, the plant literally offers them up, as its

goal is to release the produce once it has
reached maturity. Therefore, a gardener's
main responsibility when harvesting is
to be mindful of the process. A conscious gardener, even more so, will have
by observation and care
an intuitive sense of when the time
will be right. Each plant displays its own
character once its produce is ripe for picking. The handling and preparing of this produce are different for each plant. Therefore,
one must know one's garden and its tendencies intimately. Simply pay attention.

One of the focuses of this book has been on encouraging you
to cooperate and, in many senses, communicate with your plants.
Notice the plant's changes. Any differences in color, position,
texture, or vibrancy can signal the time for harvest. While some
plants continue to live and produce, many wilt after fruiting.
Know what you are dealing with, and be aware of its activity.
When fruit or vegetables appear on the plant, do not be too hasty
in picking them from the stem. Depending on the produce, there
may be best times for optimal taste and nutritional value. This will
also affect what you want to do with the produce immediately
after harvest.

For instance, if you know you will want to eat it immediately,
make sure the fruit is ripe. However, if you would like to store
some or eat it over a period of time, you may choose to pick your
produce at earlier developmental stages, as they will continue to
ripen even off the stem. A good example of this is bananas. One
may purchase a bundle of bananas before they are ripe for the purpose of having bananas over a period of days. If picked strategi-
cally, a fresh, ripe banana would be available every day if variably
ripe ones are eaten sequentially. Also, you may have preferences for
the taste of a vegetable at certain stages. For instance, for taste and

texture differences, tomatoes are often harvested while nearly ripe but still green.

The only real dangers to the plant during harvest are the following:

- **Overharvesting:** Taking more than needed of the developing produce can change the behavior of the plant, offsetting its natural development. In most cases, however, overharvesting is not deadly.

- **Rough handling:** Breaking the plant's stem, uprooting the plant, or roughly removing vegetation in a manner that damages the plant is the most common mistake and can lead to a plant's death.

- **Premature harvesting:** Picking the produce before it is ready is not typically fatal to the plant. However, it can make it easier to damage the plant, or, at minimum, early picking can significantly decrease the quality of taste and texture.

- **Failure to harvest:** Leaving produce on the plant for too long is also a common mistake, as new gardeners may not always know when they have left fruit on the plant for too long, and as a result, it falls to the ground. Normally, this does not have a detrimental effect on the plant—in fact, this would be the natural process in the wild—but you will lose valuable produce. Also, this can create a situation where unwanted insects and animals are attracted to the garden. This can cause not only invasion of the healthy plant but also mold, rot, and other fungal or microbial infestation.

Each of these actions (or inactions) can cause problems to the plants in their own ways. The key, again, is to know what you are dealing with and what works best for the plant. If the gardener stays in tune with the activity and growth of their plants, there will be nothing to worry about. In fact, your spiritual engagement with the plants should make it easier to anticipate when and how to harvest.

»»»» NOURISHING MEDITATION ««««

For this meditation, it is recommended that you go into your garden, or at least sit where your garden is visible. If you like, feel free to sit with your eyes closed in whatever space you choose, as you usually would. However, the sight of your plants, whether indoors or out-doors, may enhance the experience. Get comfortable and face your plants, or sit among them if you are outdoors. Relax your gaze and just look out at your surroundings. Stare blankly, as if daydreaming, while maintaining awareness of the life around you.

Begin in the normal fashion by following your breath. If you are choosing to do this with your eyes open, it may be more challenging to visualize the breath, but do not be concerned with this. Just mentally track the air flow as it enters your nose, fills your body, and is released back out through the nose. Breathe fully, using your diaphragm, and exhale with a little gentle force with the intention of releasing all the air within. Once you find a rhythm with your diaphragm and airflow, keep it going for five to seven deep belly breaths. Let the sensation of your breath wash over you. Slowly release your diaphragm on your inhala-tions, as if to invite the outside air into your inner spaces.

If you are performing this meditation in the presence of your plants, be aware of the subtle transaction between you and them. Recognize that they too are breathing alongside you and that in breathing together, you are nourishing each other. There is a unity in this simple act, a connection. Breathe out as if you are joyfully giving your breath to your garden. Breathe in with gratitude, not rushing or forcing the inhalation; rather, take it in with awareness.

After doing a few rounds of this, continue to breathe deeply and stay with the energy of the moment. Shift your attention to the condi-tion of your plants. Passively look them over while keeping your gaze relaxed. Recognize their growth. Remember their journey. Did you pick them from a store or greenhouse and plant them in your soil? Did you start them from seed? When was the first time you met this plant?

Remain in a meditative mind state. Do not try to actively engage these memories or think about the questions too hard. Just hear or read them and let your mind play as it wants. You may see images of picking out your plants, or memories of placing them in the earth. There may be a special moment or image of your garden that comes to mind, like a time when you were watering and the setting sunlight gleamed off the water droplets on your plants in a beautiful way. You may recall the first time a flower or vegetable bulb popped out. Whatever it may be for you, let the mind show you these special moments. While staying mindful of your breath exchange with your garden, let your heart fill with the tenderness and love exchanged in these moments. Maybe you are not used to thinking of your plants in this way, but take this time to appreciate the relationship that you have had with them.

While in this moment of stillness and silence, let us introduce a phrase to use as a mantra for the remainder of the meditation. Inwardly say, "I am life, and I gratefully share myself with you." Although you are encouraged to remain silent, it can also be fulfilling to speak this to your plants directly if you are in the garden. Even in silence, project these words to your surroundings. Continue to repeat this phrase with each deep breath for a few moments. Try to give yourself the time it takes to complete seven breaths in this way. It does not matter if your mind decides to repeat this phrase slowly or rapidly during your breathing. Just remain in control of the rhythm, inhaling and exhaling at a slow, deep pace. "I am life, and I gratefully share myself with you."

Once you have done this, release the mantra and relax your breathing, allowing it to find its own natural rhythm. Sit in silence for a little while, feeling the peaceful energy that you have invited into the space. Inwardly bow to yourself and honor this time of nourishment, gratitude, and love. You have supported and nourished these plants from day one. By spending a little time in recognition of your role in their life, you are tuning yourself to a beautiful frequency. Be aware of this, and present in the current moment. When you feel comfortable, release the meditation. It is recommended that you just sit for a while in appreciation of your garden, as well as your own hand in it. Be thankful for being on this journey toward deeper connection and self-realization. Be thankful for the blessing and positive energy of your garden.

CHAPTER 8
WISDOM OF AYURVEDA

"The Lord hath created medicines out of the earth;
and he that is wise will not abhor them."

—*Ecclesiasticus 38:4*

In order to reach these higher realizations about gardening—or anything else, for that matter—one must first realize oneself. There are many paths to doing so, but very few have the continuous proven lineage of understanding life that Ayurveda possesses. Ayurveda provides the perfect framework, as it incorporates these heavy spiritual philosophies alongside the mundane concerns of diet, health, and behavior. By now, you have been exposed to a lot of information about this. Some of it has been practical, action-based information, while some has served a philosophical purpose. However, it all comes together within Ayurveda.

This is not to discount other belief systems or philosophies, but one would be hard-pressed to find a teaching that includes all these factors. The intention here is that by gaining even a passive understanding of Ayurveda, one might internalize and apply its wisdom to one's gardening practice and, through that, enhance one's overall life experience.

Several of the topics and techniques covered throughout this book are aligned with Ayurveda, even if they are not explicitly spiritual in nature. It behooves us to now get clear on exactly what Ayurveda is and why it will help improve our gardening and, by way of the garden, our life.

Ayurveda means "the science of life." (In Sanskrit, *ayur* means "life," and *veda* is "science" or "knowledge.") In essence, this philosophy represents a way of understanding all things about what it means to be human. From the subtle to the richly physical, Ayurveda is a path to understanding what the human being is and how we should interact with our environment. It is this interaction that applies specifically to gardening. First, let's gain an understanding of the science itself.

Ayurveda is a medical science from ancient India that goes back more than 5,000 years. It is largely based on herbalism, but as a holistic science, it incorporates mind, body, and spirit. This way of life teaches us many things, not the least of which is how to interact with and use our environment. This science puts one in touch with one's inner witness, the one within that perceives all and processes life from the deepest levels of being. Even without reaching a deep enlightenment from Ayurveda, one can greatly improve one's health just by taking on the attitude toward life that Ayurveda teaches.

Though there are different schools of thought within Ayurveda, they all come down to a few core principles. These, known as the Shad Darshan, or the Six Philosophies of Life, comprise the commonly accepted foundation of modern Ayurveda:

- ❁ **Sankhya:** The truth of life; a cosmological understanding of consciousness and the manifestation of the universe.

- ❁ **Nyāya:** Realization through logic.

- **Vaisheshika:** The atomic theory of existence; knowledge of the detailed components of life.
- **Mīmāṃsā:** Ritual and manipulation of matter or action to attain self-knowledge.
- **Yoga:** Union; harmonious cooperation of mind, body, spirit, environment, and so on. Uses breathing techniques, poses, and other methodology to unify a human being with the divine.
- **Vedanta:** Literally, "ending of knowledge"—achievement of oneness. Philosophy concerned with understanding consciousness as a whole and the ultimate relationship between the self and the universe.

Many people also include elements of Buddhism (including the Four Noble Truths and concepts of self-realization), as Ayurveda and Buddhism are aligned with the same truths and are synergistic in every way.[61]

While many philosophies flow together as a cohesive foundation for the science of Ayurveda, the most relevant to this discussion are Sankhya, Vaisheshika, and Vedanta. They stand out because they deal directly with the relationship between consciousness and the physical world.

⟫⟫⟫ SANKHYA ⟪⟪⟪

Sankhya theory rests on the idea that all of reality arises from a unified consciousness field, otherwise known as the source, the foundation of the universe. It is for this reason that consciousness is said to dwell in everything and connect all things. We have touched on this subject in chapter 5, where we discussed prana to illustrate how reality is made of sheaths or coverings over this source consciousness. Ninth-century Vedic sage Adi Shankara taught on this subject the most extensively. According to his model, there are nine *koshas*, or sheaths, by which we experience reality. Those are as follows, from the mundane to the innermost spiritual:

61 Vasant Lad, *Textbook of Ayurveda: A Complete Guide to Clinical Assessment* (Albuquerque: Ayurvedic Press, 2007).

- Environmental (extended body)
- Personal physical body
- Prana body (vital energy)
- Mind
- Intellect
- Ego
- Personal soul
- Collective soul
- Universal soul

Each of these layers of consciousness carries a vital part of what makes us complete beings, and the same can be said for any life-form. Though life manifests in different stages of complexity, all beings are believed to exist in this way. For the purposes of understanding this through gardening, the most relevant koshas are the environmental, personal physical body, prana body, and universal soul. The environmental kosha is relevant because our gardens and all of nature would be included in this notion of the extended body.

It is healthy for us to cultivate the understanding that what you see in nature, by way of its relationship to your being, is inseparable and therefore a part of you. What is breathing without the plants acting as outer lungs, transforming your exhalation into a nourishing inhalation? How do you move without ground to stand on? Can you see without the light of day providing the opportunity to perceive? The answers to these questions and the like should lead you to the conclusion that the codependency of your senses and logic on the outside world necessitates that they, the consciousness and its environment, be thought of as one happening. In the act of gardening, you are not just the gardener but also the way by which a magnificent garden comes into the world.

In regard to your personal body, it is considered the *anna maya kosha*, which in Sanskrit means "layer made of food." In Ayurveda, it is taught that the physical body is merely a collection of nutritional building blocks derived from the food we eat. In other words, "You are what you eat," or, more accurately, "Your body is made of what you ate." This is vital to how we are encouraged to relate to our food and the kinds of nutritional choices we make.

We will discuss in the chapter on prana (chapter 9) how the vital energy is part of the overall being of a human. As the animating force within each cell and thought, prana is transferred and communicated through the food we eat, the environment and phenomena. It is the necessary life breath of all beings and is shared between the individual and the whole. This whole includes nature and your plants. This layer of energy is thought to be just as much a part of you as your physical body. Every living thing has prana. When we eat, we take in the prana of our food. This prana becomes part of the makeup of your own prana body. This is especially important in gardening, because the energy of your food can be skillfully considered and used for the best results in your health and well-being.

Also, the universal layer of consciousness holds importance because it is the connection point between you and the plants you are growing. Realizing your oneness with other living beings is a major goal of most spiritual systems. We may be on a unique journey in applying this concept to gardening, but achieving unity is the objective. If this concept is made real and incorporated into your life, even if only on an intellectual level, it can be transcendent to your experience of self and others.

It is not the intention of this book to grant the reader full self-awareness. However, if these discussions and practices can point the way, it is well served. This aspect of Ayurveda is spoken of in a more philosophical sense here. Just remain open to the idea that at the very ground of your being, you and all the living beings of nature come from the same source. This idea is central to Ayurveda. This multilayered model itself is not Sankhya philosophy, but it is closely related when doing self-analysis and understanding the connections between the self and the outer world. Therefore, we can place a pin in this for now and consider it to be the breakdown of the individual, whereas Sankhya is the universal version of this understanding.

To fully understand Sankhya philosophy, we must cover the creation story of all manifestations. This is not a linear creation story in the same sense as those found in the Bible or other religious texts. Although scientific in some senses, this story is not objective or materialistic either, as some scientific models of creation may appear. What makes Sankhya unique is that it is believed to be an ongoing, ever-unfolding creation happening every moment of life. Think of it as more of a "how" explanation than a time-bound historical answer to "When?" or "What?" This is the Vedic understanding of how things come into manifestation from the same pure source. Vedic tradition refers to this ultimate truth as Brahma, the absolute unity of all manifest and unmanifest reality.

In Sankhya philosophy, all life experience springs from the first duality, that of purusha, or pure consciousness, and prakriti, the creative potential or primordial matter of the universe. The original state of dualism is thought to sprout from the pure universal awareness, Brahma, as a way of giving this consciousness the experience of life and activity. As it is pure oneness itself, it would not otherwise have experience.

This division at the beginning of all creation in every moment is echoed in the creation of new plant life. In this sense, one can think of the seed as purusha and the soil, the elements, and so on as prakriti. *Purusha* is a Sanskrit word that essentially means "the consciousness that dwells in the city of the senses." (*Pur* means "city," and *sheta* means "living" or "dwelling.") *Prakriti*, in Sanskrit, conveys many meanings. Ultimately, it means "creative potential" or "essential nature." Wherever it is used, it references the nature or potential out of which something is expressed. In this book, you will see it used in both ways, here meaning the primordial "stuff" that all things are formed from, and later, when speaking of the doshas, meaning one's own elemental constitution, or Ayurvedic DNA. This seed of purusha enters the ripe soil and conditions of prakriti, and their union forms the manifest creation.

Through a series of outgrowths from this union, the universe and all its effects come into being—first, the intelligence that governs the proper placement of all parts of the universe, then the individual points of view known as the ego, or "I am," of every living creature, and from this individuated experience comes the gunas. Consider them to be the universal qualities that permeate all creation, the result of universal consciousness being confined to an individual experience. These gunas are sattva, rajas, and tamas. In a simplified concept, the gunas are the options of experience afforded to consciousness once it has merged with material reality. *Sattva* is Sanskrit for "pure perception," *rajas* is the movement of awareness or action, and *tamas* is linked to inertia, darkness, and inactivity.

Though these words may seem foreign, do not feel overwhelmed. Just think about it: If you were a completely alone and unique eternal being, what would you do? First, in order to experience anything, you would have to become plural, if not a multitude, in order to know others and have something to do. Because the reality is still one indivisible whole, however, this game of experience is an illusion and must come through a separation of the awareness of unity into a perceived duality—the "I am this and you are that" awareness of every individual ego.

On its own, this consciousness would have only the three gunas as options for activity: either to be still in its own awareness of self and perceive the whole works, to do something, or to do nothing in an inert way, like sleep or even death. The significance here is not so much in having an in-depth understanding of the gunas, but more so in knowing what these modes of action and inaction create when turned on each other.

Sankhya teaches that the active rajas principle, when turned toward sattva, creates the five senses and their actions. In other words, activity within pure perception differentiates into sensual experience. This is an Ayurvedic understanding of why we see, hear, smell, taste, and touch. It is the consciousness, living within the body, making use of the available five portals of perception into the outer world. This also manifests what we call mind, the interpretive processing agent of consciousness. When rajas acts on tamas, the result is the inorganic world of objects, which at its foundation is represented by the five elements of space, air, fire, water, and earth.

If this work were focused on Sankhya, there could be a lot more said about the philosophy and its relevance to Ayurveda. However, for our purposes, Sankhya is important because it shows a basic mapping of how consciousness comes into being in the material world. Invest what you will in the truth of this concept, but its usefulness lies in its applicability to all life. This is said to be a shared truth for all conscious beings, and its implications have stood the test of time and much scrutiny as a way of understanding. It is from the resulting elements and senses that the doshas and all other Ayurvedic teachings arise.

This is how Sankhya can be understood and applied to the garden. First, in understanding that your plants are another form or version of this same activity, that they too are universal consciousness experiencing reality through a different mode and expression. Even more profound, your experience of them is based on the belief that you are separate, when in reality you and your garden are both a part of one actual event, which is the source experiencing gardening.

Second, Sankhya brings us the concept of doshas and the five elements as necessary components of manifestation. The importance of this is exhibited through our application of this knowledge in choosing our foods and how we care for our gardens. The next section will cover some of the applications of the doshas to gardening. Just understand that the basic principles of doshic theory are based on the five elements of nature.

These familiar elements are recognized in other holistic systems of health and spirituality, albeit sometimes with slight alterations. The elements of nature are perceived in Ayurveda as space, air, fire, water, and earth. Traditional Chinese medicine also uses natural elements to understand the human body and experience. However, in this system the five elements consist of wood, metal, fire, earth, and water. These alternative categories still embody the same universal qualities. However, these different classifications open other doorways of understanding and deserve mention. Ayurveda, in accordance with Sankhya theory, uses the elements to describe aspects of human experience and nature.

⟫⟫⟫ VAISHESHIKA ⟪⟪⟪

As an aspect of Ayurveda, Vaisheshika supports Sankhya philosophy. Where Sankhya introduces and explains the appearance of the elements, Vaisheshika deals more intimately with them. This conceptualization of the elements is more scientific in its approach. In fact, Vaisheshika may be one of the earliest scientific models for the theory of atoms. Vedic texts on Vaisheshika theory, dated as early as the ninth century BCE, describe the elements as being composed of tiny, invisible atoms that the elements as we perceive are an amalgamation of.

In other words, when we perceive earth, on an atomic level, it is really fire, water, air, and space atoms as well. We experience it as earth because it has more earth atoms within the molecule than the others. This way of looking at the elements, and therefore all of life, was revolutionary and opened the doorway to much of the medicinal knowledge exhibited in Ayurveda to the present day. It is through this branch that Ayurveda includes the gunas, or qualities, of each element and their pairings, known as doshas. At this point, you have seen brief references to doshas, but now we will get to know them.

First, the elements! This particular set of five elements should be familiar. Space, air, fire, water, and earth have long been considered the building blocks of material reality. What may be new to you is the understanding of the relevance of these elements to you, including nonphysical dimensions.

Before I expound on these, there are a few other elements to mention regarding Vaisheshika. The philosophy includes nine causative factors for all experiences: the five aforementioned elements and time, direction, soul, and mind. Our focus is on the five elements, but the importance of these other four is worthy of mention. These are some of the important reasons these causative factors are relevant, not only in Ayurveda but also in gardening.

- **Time:** Measures change, related to dosha functions and behaviors, allows awareness of Earth's activities, and related to psychological processes such as memory, meditative states, and experience.

- **Direction:** Used to understand doshic behavior and function (particularly *vata*, directional movement), magnetic position in relation to Earth's poles, effects on material reality and living beings, and energetic qualities and their associations based on spacing (for example, feng shui and intuitive decorating).

- **Soul:** Considered to be the source of consciousness within a being. In Vaisheshika, there is the universal soul and the individual soul, though they are one, with different perspectives. The concept is that the soul's presence is responsible for the emergence of consciousness; therefore, it is a causative factor in all manifestations.

- **Mind:** Included as a causative factor due to its irreducible nature as the director of experience. It points awareness in particular directions and processes the input of the senses.

Each of these factors has obvious correlations to a conscious gardening project. Examples follow:

- **Time:** Timing of seeding and care for plants.
- **Direction:** Placement of particular plants in their most agreeable settings for sun exposure, soil, and water access, as well as energy, and so on.
- **Soul:** Your attention and awareness of the garden, tending to its needs and upkeep, enjoying, and energy-enriching spiritual time and presence in the garden.
- **Mind:** Use of ingenuity and skill in care of the garden.

The science of Ayurveda is founded on an understanding of the elements as having not only physical qualities but also characteristics that correlate with psychological concepts. Also, each element is said to harness a specific kind of energy. Vaisheshika gave Ayurveda its understanding of all these secrets of the elements and their special relationships within the universe. These qualities follow:

❀ **Space:** The empty, ever-expanding vastness in which all material things appear—associated with sound and vibration, as space is the most necessary component for sound to occur. This ether element is said to contain nuclear energy and is thought to be the first elemental expression of consciousness. Its vibration is love and omnipotence.

❀ **Air:** The air or wind element occurs when that consciousness moves. It is intrinsically linked to prana, which is discussed in chapter 9. Ayurveda considers air to be responsible for all movement, including actions you may not consider air related—blood flow, nervous system activity, peristalsis, and so on. It is concerned with movement in a particular direction and associated with electrical energy.

❀ **Fire:** Ayurveda teaches that all transformative actions in nature are qualitatively or literally fire-related activities, including metabolic processes—even digestion of information or other psychological effects. Its energy is radiance and therefore naturally associated with brilliance, luminosity, intellect, and perception. Fire serves as an excellent example for the kind of correlative, holistic science that Ayurveda employs with the elements. For example, the sharp, penetrating character of fire is also applied to sharpness of mind and having a forceful or convincing personality. Medical and dietary advice can be administered based on conceptualizing these personality traits as fire. This fire association allows Ayurveda to contain some simple logic and experience that can have value in caring for medical conditions. For instance, inflammation is considered fire—consider the expression "My skin is on fire." Ayurveda would recommend cooling, water-promoting treatments for that fire inflammation.

❀ **Water:** Ayurveda places a lot of importance on water for its cohesive qualities, as well as its unique feature as a universal solvent. All living creatures contain water, and it connects everything through this universal assimilation. Considered the most necessary element for life to occur, it is associated with the sense of taste and contains chemical energy. Understanding these qualities of water has helped shape the invention of medicines and recognition of their effects on the body. The physical world contains a lot of water, but Ayurveda also considers anything that exhibits similar qualities to be of the nature of water. Characteristics such as cool, liquid, slimy, or oily are identified as properties of water. Therefore, any thing or person showing these qualities would be said to be of high water content.

❀ **Earth:** The sages of Ayurveda identified this element with all dense, firm, solid things. Earth is responsible for mechanical energy, and its structural qualities take on mental and physical truths. It is the presence of earth in the body that enables us to grow bones, hair, teeth, and nails. The earth element is normally associated with the sense of smell.

The information that Vaisheshika provides the Ayurvedic sciences allows for the elements and their qualities to be used in a measurable, calculated way. In cooperation with the other branches, this philosophy has shaped much of what we know and are able to do with Ayurveda to this day.

>>>>> VEDANTA <<<<<

The gift of Vedanta is its philosophical contribution to Ayurveda. In this teaching, there is an emphasis on consciousness and the underlying oneness of all things. It is through Vedanta that we know much of the information provided by Ayurveda about consciousness, awareness, presence, clarity, meditation, and so on. In many ways, it is a specific study of consciousness itself; however, it is nonscientific in nature. Many teachings from Vedanta come through direct observation and inquiry. Despite the subjective nature of this wisdom, it allows Ayurveda to provide effective therapy and understanding on a subject that many sciences tend to steer away from. Self-realization and related topics can therefore be simplified and dealt with in a practical way with verifiable results. This ability is thanks to the contributions of Vedanta.

As stated earlier, all six philosophies contribute something vital to the overall science of Ayurveda. However, Sankhya, Vaisheshika, and Vedanta all relate directly to spiritual gardening as they deal with material reality and understanding consciousness outside of the human being. For review, we can consider the following donations of these teachings to the subject at hand:

- **Sankhya:** Identification of universal consciousness and model for transformation of consciousness, from the subtle to the gross expression of life. This provides us with an understanding of how we and our plants can come from the same source. Using this concept helps us build a deeper connection to the process of growth in our plants and an appreciation for the unfolding of the life process.

- **Vaisheshika:** Scientific understanding and model for the material universe according to the elements. Accounts for temperaments, characteristics, and relationships among the elements. In understanding these truths, we can manipulate and work with nature in a more harmonious way. Many of the practical applications of Ayurveda to the garden, our diet choices, and medicine is based on the contributions of this branch of Ayurveda.

- **Vedanta:** Understanding of consciousness, opening the possibilities of unity and communication with others on a deeper level of awareness. In terms of using the garden as a tool toward spiritual attainment, Vedanta is an essential concept. It provides legitimacy to the meditative processes and mindfulness practices that are designed for building bonds of love and awareness with your plants. If there were not any discoveries around consciousness or how it operates, connecting with nature in this way wouldn't be possible.

CHAPTER 9

PLANTS AS MESSENGERS OF PRANA

UNIVERSAL INTELLIGENCE: THOUGHTS, ENERGY, AND EMOTION AS TRANSLATED PRANA

"Plants give us oxygen for the lungs and for the soul."
—*Linda Solegato*

Most often, when we consider the beginnings of life, one looks toward the origins of humanity. However, let us consider that if we follow a purely scientific tract, the first biological organism would have had to necessarily be preceded by some form of plant life, if for no other reason than for there to be a food source. Eukaryotic cells do not need any other nutrient source than the natural elements of sun, soil, and water to thrive. Animal life, on the other hand, must eat something else within a food chain that ultimately starts with some sort of plant.

Plants are truly the progenitors of life on this planet. When one steps back and surveys the natural environment of Earth in a detached sense, the plants are the number one most important form of life. Our human ego may want to argue against this point, but all life depends on the plant kingdom. No other organisms depend solely on human beings to thrive. On the contrary, if all human beings on the planet were separated from nature, it would thrive, whereas the plant kingdom is integral to the process of life on this planet. Its importance and contributions cannot be measured. Understanding this, maybe one should look to the first signs of plant life for our true origins.

If we consider ourselves to be consciousness, as taught by many Eastern sciences, as opposed to this human biological form, we can trace the origins of life way farther back in time. In the Vedic and Tantric systems of ancient India, life begins with the insertion of consciousness-carrying prana into the form. With that said, life also leaves a body once prana has left. This *prana* is the vital energy, the life breath of every living thing on this planet. There is also cosmic prana acting on the planet itself as it participates in the universal drama of planets, solar systems, and other heavenly bodies. Bits of information and awareness from all *prana* are deposited in every respirating creature, including ourselves.

Imagine being a witness to the very first moment of respiration on this planet. In many spiritual traditions, there is mention of the importance of the breath in human life, physiological and spiritual. For this life-giving prana to begin circulating on this planet, something had to breathe in and then out, and since then, there has been this drama. This life-form would have definitely been a plant, by most scientific evolutionary standards. This proverbial Tree of Life would have marked the first terrestrial life on Earth. Even if we consider the prehistoric oceanic life, plants would come before animal life. From the moment that the first eukaryotic organism "breathed," this planet has given rise to countless biological beings. It is the plant's ability to sustain on pure sunlight, transforming it into edible and breathable prana, that makes it such a blessing. Life as we know it on this planet could not have come into being, let alone sustained itself, without the contributions of the plant world. Through another lens, we might look at this as a divine act, as described in the Bible: "And the Lord God formed man of the dust of the ground, and breathed into his nostrils the breath of life, and man became a living soul."[62]

This same "breath of life" is in all creatures. It is prana. The ever-flowing exchange of energy and inspiration within the living world. The driving force behind all animation, vibration, and movement in the universe. This is what is being spoken of when one uses the term *prana*.

That first exhalation by plant life carried within it the very building blocks of all other biological existence. This plant, by way of the energy of the sunlight, the nutrient-rich waters within the Earth, and some form of consciousness that knew what to do with it all, pulled carbon dioxide in, processed it, and produced enough oxygen to release it to a budding new world. Although this is a romanticized depiction, one must marvel at the moment. Only consciousness could cause such a miracle. Even when seen as a beneficent random occurrence, in the most deterministic scientific sense, this was a paramount point for life itself on this planet. Is it possible that all living beings carry some genetic imprint of gratitude for this? A desire to live in harmony and dependence on plants felt by all of nature?

Some might say it is we biological forms that serve the plants, selecting and disseminating their seed throughout the Earth, helping their evolution and growth. Indeed, it is a mutual relationship of life and health. It is in shifting this perspective that we might arrive at a more respectful and loving relationship with our garden. The garden is humanity's controlled version of the natural world. Tamed for the purpose of food production, medicine, and visual aesthetic, a garden is a unique creation of humankind. It is a testament to the ability of humans to live in harmony and cooperation with the environment. It is one thing to go foraging through a forest or field for these kinds of benefits, but it is a completely different experience to cultivate them.

---

62 Biblica, Song of Gen. 2:7.

Nature has given us everything we
need to live as long and as strong as we
are intended to. When one experiences
wild, untamed nature, eating of its
fruits, watching its activity, learning its
secrets, a different part of the human
spirit is reached. Feelings of support,
harmony, synchronicity, balance,
and sustainability are experienced, as

the world appears to prop up your very existence. This is a natural
product of prana. When one creates a garden and tends to it, they are
putting themselves back in touch with this pranic relationship, giving
and receiving, cultivating growth in cooperation with the planet and
its elements. This is natural to the human soul.

HOW A PLANT STORES ENERGY,
⟫⟫⟩ PHYTONUTRIENTS, PRANA ⟨⟨⟨⟨

The beauty and complexity of nature is not accidental. Nor is your
ability to perceive it. The human organism has exactly the right nervous system and consciousness to perceive the world that we know.
Other biological life sees this world in other spectrums and levels
of activity. Even though human sciences have largely discounted its
sophistication, the consciousness present within plant life must also
perceive the world differently.

Even among humans, there are differences in perception and
opinion. All of life has its own unique front row seat to this universe.
As stated in the Brihadaranyaka Upanishad, verse 2.2.20, "Just as
a spider spins a thread and as sparks come forth from fire, similarly,
all breaths, all worlds, all deities, and all beings arise from the Self.
Its secret meaning is the Truth of truth. The Breath is the Real made
manifest and the Self is the reality of the Breath."[63]

---

63 Swāmī Mādhavānanda, *Brihadaranyaka Upanishad* (Howrah, India: Advaita Ashram, 2018)

Clearly, the breath is more than just respiration and transference of air molecules. The breath, also known as prana, must be integral to the actual experience of life, not just the animation of it. So, what does this tell us? What is consciousness? How does it work? What exactly does prana have to do with it?

In most ancient contexts, prana is associated with air or the wind. As we know from Ayurveda, this kind of classification is not always about the actual composition of a thing, but rather its characteristics. When prana is spoken of as wind, it is the moving, energizing principle of prana that is being described. Similarly, and maybe more accurately, prana is sometimes associated with electricity. Electricity is also characterized with wind in many old elemental sciences of the world, and therefore you will see it and prana often spoken of interchangeably. This energizing, present force in all life contains within it a kind of information that promotes and creates health within the organism.

Though all creatures share in this global prana, what happens with it once it is internalized may differ. This is where consciousness plays a role. The relationship between consciousness and prana is akin to a computer and an electronic signal, respectively. The message travels, carrying with it information that the computer processes. Each living being has its own nervous system and mind-body processing unit, complete with its own quirks, nuances, thoughts, behaviors, and appetites. The prana receives, stimulates and animates the mind-body to action, thoughts, and behaviors particular to its own design and purpose. This energy can be channeled for multiple purposes, though the source of it is the same for all.

In the natural physical world, our best example of this action is the Sun. Solar prana, while it is seen as only one particular kind, is an excellent illustration of what prana is and how it works. The energy of the Sun provides us with so much: vibrational and gravitational energy, temperature effects, radiance, electrical energy—you name it. The Sun is ultimately the source.

On more subtle levels, this source is within the living beings of the world and is responsible for the life experience of those organisms and is known through the ancient wisdom traditions as consciousness, the self. The parallels between the Sun and the light of consciousness have been lauded by humanity since the dawn of time. The relevance here is in understanding the relational connection between light and thoughts. Both emanatie from their source as prana. This subtle energy is transformed to information, as it provides the consciousness with something to react to, process, and integrate. There is a code of information and action that affects all that can receive it. This code is held within prana. The Mundaka Upanishad, verse 3.1.4, states, "Truly, it is Breath that pervades all beings. Knowing it, the wise person does not speak of anything else. Reveling in the Self, delighting in the Self, and performing work, such a person is the greatest of the knowers of the Absolute."[64]

For plants, this life force may be directed at strengthening cell walls, leaf or stem growth, supporting the root system, or producing flowers for reproduction. As a plant takes in prana, it stores it within its body as complex sugar bonds. This process, aided by the cosmic prana of the Sun, helps the plant to do everything it needs to survive.

Many plants also use this prana to create natural chemicals just as our bodies contain a sea of biochemical processes. These chemicals, called phytonutrients, which the plant is creating out of its own prana for its own benefit, once consumed can serve the human body-mind complex very well. Phytonutrients are usually created by the plant as protective measures or as growth-promoting adaptations. There are tens of thousands of known phytonutrients, and surely many more undiscovered. Of these, certain particular phytonutrients have caught the attention of the medical community. Carotenoids, flavonoids, and phytoestrogens are all being heavily studied for their antioxidant, anti-inflammatory, and cancer-fighting benefits. The noteworthy discovery of these chemicals has been very useful, thus far, and with further study may hold vast medical advancements for humans in the future.

---

64 S. Sitarama Sastri, *The Isa, Kena, & Mundaka Upanishads and Sri Sankara's Commentary*, translated by S. Sitarama (G. A. Natesan & Co., Printers & Publishers, 1905).

Phytonutrients are of particular interest because they point the way to a deeper realization of what prana is and possibly how it works. They also can be seen as evidence of a kind of consciousness present in the plants. When we analyze a phytonutrient, we are separating out a chemical that, unlike vitamins and minerals, is not a building block or an essential part of the plant's biochemical composition. These essentially are produced as adaptations of the plant to its environment. Insect repellents, pigment control, UV protection—all are examples of what the plant deals with through its phytonutrients. It is likely that we are just scratching the surface of understanding how these processes work and why. Regardless, a consciousness, even at the most passive base level of awareness, is responsible for producing and regulating the amount and content of phytonutrients found within the plant. Outside of the literal biochemical benefits of ingesting these nutrients, there is a subtle transference of prana due to this link of consciousness.

If one looks at prana not so much as a detectable, physical thing but more as an energetic intelligence, the whole production from start to finish can be viewed accordingly. A human being, when eating a fruit or vegetable, is taking in not only the vitamins and minerals from the body of the plant but also the products of this plant's living consciousness. In effect, this is a small transference of the plant's consciousness, a biochemical code or message, and quite possibly the connection to how healthy plants and their produce help create healthy human beings.

If we cultivate this understanding of our plants as messengers bringing little gift packets of life energy, then we can see how important it is to respect and nurture them. When you harvest from a plant, you take its stored prana into your own body. By living in close quarters, as well as making a practice of intentionally breathing with them, you are also directly exchanging this prana. Even though this is always occurring naturally, placing more awareness and attention on this relationship will cause it to grow. This energy exchange can be realized as more than just a transaction of breath.

In the more subtle dimensions of awareness, these exchanges can be experienced with more significance. Ayurveda teaches us that every thought, breath, sight, food, drink, or experience is received, processed, and incorporated into your very makeup. Your life experiences, whether passive or intentional, are being digested by the consciousness within and utilized to either build, heal, or break down your cells. There are many further implications in this, but we can keep it to one's biological and mental aspects for now.

Staying within an Ayurvedic framework, we are taught that the total human being is composed of several koshas, or coverings. It is necessary only to understand that each of these koshas is made of what the consciousness perceives and takes to be part of its self at those levels. Analogous to an onion, with its layers, the pure consciousness is covered over, from the innermost subtle self to the gross outer lining of the body and environment, with what it consumes or perceives.

Nine such koshas were outlined by the great sage and progenitor of this theory, Adi Shankara. They are divided into groups of three, representing different levels of awareness. The first group of coverings are concerned with the physical experience. They are environmental, personal (physical), and energetic (prana) layers. The second grouping, consisting of the mind, the intellect, and the ego, is related to mental life. Last, three coverings are related to the spiritual dimensions of life: the personal soul, the collective soul, and the universal domain of consciousness. Here, the focus will be on the *prana maya kosha*, the layer made of energy.

When considering the prana of every living being, its purpose is to enliven, energize, animate, and otherwise conduct conscious energy. When a person eats, the person is assimilating the energy and composition of the food. In this way, prana becomes a huge part of the exchange. Human beings incorporate the prana energy of their food into their own energetic fields, in much the same way that the physical nutrients are broken down to create the building blocks of the human body.

Have you ever experienced a mood change after eating certain foods? Do some foods make you feel energized, while others leave you sleepy and lethargic? These are small examples, barely scratching the surface, of how the energy is transferred during digestion. This is why Ayurveda encourages us to eat freshly harvested food as often as possible—the prana content. It is believed that the prana of the vegetable slowly diminishes the longer a vegetable is away from its source, the actual plant it grew from. While you may have never considered it in this context, you can easily observe this process. A freshly picked fruit or vegetable will gradually fade and eventually rot into nothing if left lying out on the table.

All this happens without any seeming cause other than time. However, this effect is caused by what Ayurveda refers to as prana leaving the food. Modern sciences may refer to this process as oxidation. But this is just another way of saying the same thing in a less esoteric way. The biochemical composition of the food changes and degrades as the air, the *vayu* of the once-living part of the plant, escapes from its cells.

In another way, prana can be observed in foods that continue to grow or change after being separated from the plant. Consider root foods, such as ginger root, onions, and potatoes as examples. Even long after harvested, these foods hold some level of prana; otherwise, they would not continue to adapt to their circumstances. They would not sprout buds. Their color and tastes would not go through changes as they prepare to either die or begin anew. This is a sign that life, and therefore prana, is still present.

As science continues to study these phenomena, we may arrive at some scientific logical conclusions that are completely materialistic. However, as more information is gathered, it seems to only confirm this theory of prana. Whether it is called by this name or not, there is plenty of evidence to support the existence of an animating quality to life that is observable in all creatures.

Considering this, Ayurveda teaches us to account for the temperaments of the foods that we take in. The intelligence flowing through each plant is expressed differently according to many factors, not the least of which is the life experience of the plant. Has it had the right environmental factors to thrive? Has it been damaged? What other organisms does it interact with? Aside from the generalized taste classifications and physical makeup of the food, these factors are also important. And this is where prana plays a role. Also, the expression of this prana can be seen in the nature of the food.

Ayurveda has provided a framework for understanding the different energies of food and how one should approach them as medicine and sustenance. All this and more will be explored in the next chapter. For now, just understand that when you eat a food, you are taking in more than just its physical matter. The quality of the seed itself, the quality of life, experiences, and circumstances of the plant, are all wrapped up in every bite of that food. As a living being, it has reacted and grown according to its own life and consciousness.

So, along with and because of the prana in each food, the eater is affected. This effect can be because of factors such as those Ayurveda would consider, like taste, preparation, and so on, or it can simply be because of the individual eater and that person's well-being. Either way, the *prana maya kosha* (the layer of being made of prana) of the individual takes on a little piece of the energetics of whatever is eaten. Taking this into account, one should begin paying more attention to what one eats and how it affects one. Most health-minded individuals probably already think about these things on a nutritional level. What is being encouraged here is to cultivate a respect for the more subtle transaction that takes place when you eat.

Ayurveda, traditional Chinese medicine, and many other lesser-known dietary sciences and customs take the energetics of food into consideration. The field of pharmacology is definitely nothing new to human society. What fascinates and intrigues people in the modern era is how this idea of food as medicine relates and is so useful to today's healthy lifestyle. For the most part, this is still relegated to the Western medicinal concept of "I take this to deal with that." However, many of these traditional diets are proactive in nature and not sought out as a means after a disease appears. Prana cultivation and maintaining optimal well-being are very important to anyone with this goal in mind.

To this end, Ayurveda has classified certain foods as *sattvic*— having an exemplary benign nature and being the best sustenance for optimal health. These sattvic foods are said to have this quality, in part, because of the effects they have on prana. These are foods that will promote and support optimal prana levels and flow in the individual consumer, primarily because the plants that produce these foods are themselves known to have high prana levels. It is the regular eating of these foods, along with conducive lifestyle practices, that lay the groundwork for the person to experience the full benefits of prana: a clear, serene mind state, a natural joyful exuberance, groundedness, strength of body and mind, and great immunity to disease.

All of these, and more, can be observed in the living plant before the food of it is even harvested. Beautiful blooming flowers, amaz-ing eye-catching coloration, protection from pests and disease, and healthy foliage and produce are all signs of a plant with good prana. As a conscious gardener, you will start to notice the role that you play in supporting the prana in your plants. All gardeners know when their plants are happy. This beauty and healthy growth come from optimal prana levels.

Whether it is simply taking good care of your garden or even choosing to go deeper with practices like those found in this book, your role as a caretaker is more significant in this than it may appear. It is this role or relationship with your garden that is the current focus. While this may be the first time you have ever thought about it in these terms, your goal as a gardener should always be, and proba-bly always has been, to produce good prana in your foods. Through understanding this aspect of your garden, your treatment, enjoyment, and results from the garden will increase.

Simply setting the intention, while respecting the plant as a living being, can have many benefits. What is good for the plant is ultimately going to translate into the produce from it, which you and yours will consume, and this goodness will be transferred to you. It is that simple. Working with prana and being mindful of it is merely a way of being more active in the process and intentionally bringing more of it into your life. In this book, practices are laid out that relate directly to the physical care of the plants, but others focus on nurturing the spiritual connection between yourself and your garden.

In the most subtle way, you and your garden are one in this process. The seed of what will become your gardening experience and its positive benefits are all condensed into the very seed moment when you thought that it was a good idea to start one. Even earlier still, the desire was born the first time you really enjoyed the sight or smell of a garden, tasted the difference of fresh, mindfully grown produce, or admired someone else's gardening space. Maybe you got the itch from the enjoyment of playing in the dirt as a child or growing plants for a school project.

Whatever first contact you may have had, it must have stuck, because here we are, and it is not a coincidence. Is it possible that your desire to learn more and try this out was an act of universal consciousness? Prana is the animating force within the universe, carrying out these acts through inspiration and respiration in the world of forms. Therefore, it is prana acting for the sake of its own cultivation and appreciation that is powering you to digest these very words. It is not a separate force acting in the world, but a part of all of life, the literal life breath of the universe. You are a result of prana and a propagator of it, whether you are conscious of this fact or not. How much better is it to knowingly participate in the process?

Acting as a small microcosm, the garden can be a space to further attune with and understand prana. Ask yourself, "What causes a seed to grow?" This is not a question of how it works, but of why. Even if one doesn't arrive at a conclusive reason for it, marveling at the mystery has its own merits by placing attention on the unseen hand, the "magic," of the process. What differences can one observe in wild plants versus those that have been cultivated? Is there a different vibrancy? Are the fruit, foliage, and flower of one preferable? There are reasons for your opinion on either. The interconnectivity of all the elements through consciousness is powered by prana, and the results of your input should speak for itself.

Logically, it should follow that a skilled gardener's love and care would help the plant fare better than if it were left to the wild elements. Watering it routinely, pruning and picking, weeding around it, proper seeding and placement—this kind of care goes a long way toward the health of the plants. The plant and its produce, in turn, provide the best possible yield, which the gardener then partakes of for food or admires as a beautiful display. There is a reciprocal relationship of benign intention and, essentially, love being exhibited even in this surface-level aspect of gardening.

Is it not all powered and supported by the movement of prana? Isn't the whole production, from start to finish, an act carried out by consciousness, through consciousness, for the benefit of consciousness? The consciousness present in both the gardener and the seed is contributing to a literal and metaphoric outgrowth of health and well-being. Throughout the whole process, it is the breath, this subtle animating element, that unifies gardener and garden as one, as a gardening experience.

PRANAYAMA EXERCISE

Pranayama is the Yogic science of working with the inner life force through manipulation and understanding of breathwork. This collection of breathing techniques is intended to enhance and maintain one's inner and outer health, as well as foster connectedness between the human being and the universe. This science is founded on many of the philosophical ideas we have discussed in this chapter, as well as ways of using the body to experience their truths. You are encouraged to do further research on pranayama and expand your experience of these techniques. They are very helpful and can be transformative for those who are deeply connected to working with prana.

The benefits of doing pranayama are always intensified when in the presence of plants. It can be one of the most effective means of finding a palpable relationship with them. If you have a comfortable sitting spot in your garden, try performing pranayama there while keeping in mind what you have learned. This can also be done indoors by choosing a special plant to nurture. As you exhale during these exercises, your breath will be inhaled directly by the plant. In this way, you are engaging your plant or plants in an exchange of nourishment infused with the added depth of the effect breathwork has on your consciousness.

If you want to level up even further in your experience, apply a little bit of aromatherapy by doing your pranayama practice in the presence of your floral, aromatic garden plants. I have always found herbs pleasurable for this as well and less likely to irritate those with pollen sensitivities. I recommend sage, cilantro, spruce, mint, oregano, or even tomato for this kind of work. The scents of these plants tend to pair well with the freshness, balance, and clarity of mind that one hopes to achieve through pranayama. Also, oregano, mint, and spruce have medicinal bonuses of opening the airways and expectorant qualities, so they are good selections for partners in any breathwork.

Here is one such technique that is exceedingly popular among meditation enthusiasts and yogis. When paired with the natural relationship of respiration that exists between you and your plants, pranayama can become noticeably more potent. Try this technique out, and if it resonates with you, see what other prana-enhancing breaths there are for you to experience.

NADI SHODHANA

Sit in a comfortable, upright position. Slightly exaggerate the posture, straightening your back without exertion or stress. Next, take your right hand and place your pointer finger and middle finger over your third-eye region in the middle of your forehead. Hold your thumb over your right nostril with your ring and pinky fingers on your left nostril. Now, breathe out a full exhalation. Before you inhale, close off your left nostril and breathe in through your right. At the peak of your inhalation, close off your right nostril and release your breath through the left side. Inhale the next breath through your left nostril while pinching off the right. Inhale fully, then close off the left side and exhale through the right nostril.

This sequence completes a full alternate-nostril breathing cycle. It may take a little practice to perform smoothly, but it will eventually come quite naturally. It is recommended that one perform anywhere from one to seven of these breath cycles in a sitting in order to get the best effects. You can also measure them by time, but make sure you pause between sets of seven and breathe normally in order to not overload your system. This technique is powerful and is intended to equalize your inner winds.

The alternate-nostril pranayama technique is especially balancing to the mind. Most report an immediate effect when it is performed correctly. By balancing one's prana, or chi, it is possible to better harness and enhance the inner life force, providing numerous health benefits and peacefulness. As you have just learned about prana and how it is present in your experience of nature, try performing the Nadi Shodhana in your garden or near your plants.

CHAPTER 10

AYURVEDA IN THE GARDEN

"God Almighty first planted a garden. And indeed,
it is the purest of human pleasures."

—Sir Francis Bacon

Now that we have covered some foundational topics in Ayurveda,
let's turn our focus toward applying these principles to our gardening
hobby and diet. As we learned in the previous chapters, Ayurveda is a
science of the elements. All uses of Ayurvedic knowledge have some
application to the natural elements, within and outside of the body. It
is believed that these five elements of space, air, fire, water, and earth
are present in everything in physical existence. As they all have their
own characteristics, these elements form particular bonds and have
certain effects. Each individual element also displays specific behavior
and reactions that can be understood for our well-being and health.
With this information, we can treat our food as medicine and care
for the plants of our gardens in ways that are evolutionary to us and
harmonious with nature.

In previous chapters, we have touched on what the five elements are and some of their properties. Now, we will go a little deeper into our understanding of them and their behaviors. To fully appreciate the science of Ayurveda, one has to recognize the elements as more than physical matter. Each of the elements is thought of as energy at different levels or vibrations. This energy is the pure light of consciousness. Originating from the source, this energy undergoes changes and behaves in different ways according to the intelligence within it.

The commonly held story of how material reality came to be begins with this source, the unmanifested, undifferentiated state of consciousness, in which the potential for all things exists, yet no thing is. Our understanding of this state of being can only be inferred through wisdom or states of meditative awareness. It must be experienced to be even slightly understood, and there are no words to fully explain it. For these reasons and many others, consciousness has been elusive to science and our usual means of attaining knowledge.

What we can gather is that we are speaking of pure potentiality—essentially, the stuff that everything can be made from, yet it doesn't originate from anything other than itself. It just is. The subject is so mysterious that many brilliant minds and spiritual giants have pondered over its properties and existence for centuries of human development, yet we still know extraordinarily little about consciousness, let alone the conscious source of all consciousness.

As it has been passed down through the wisdom traditions of the East, this infinite vastness of pure potential energy and information vibrated out the sound "*aum*" at some point before time began. Space or ether, the first element, had to be present, as space is necessary for sound to manifest. There are different thoughts on what came first and how, but for our purposes, let's assume that space and the sound "*aum*" manifested simultaneously. "*Aum*" is considered the pranava, or cosmic sound, in Vedic teaching because it is believed to be the subtle vibration within the universal consciousness from which all reality springs.

Continuing with our elemental origin story, this subtle energy of space moved within its infinite self, and this movement created air. Air, being rough and dry, created friction in its movements; this friction manifested heat and light, which intensified into fire. As the heat of the fire cooled and dissipated, the energy liquified into what we know as water. This water energy continued to slow down and lose heat, eventually becoming solid, and the earth element was born. From the earth element, all solid physical manifestations, including living beings, are formed, and the stage is set for life as we know it.

While this may be an allegorical explanation for the creation of the elements, the truth that it shares is this idea of energy passing from the pure source down to even the soil, and that this relationship acts as a continuum of consciousness throughout. In this concept, all the elements are rooted in consciousness, and therefore they are much more than just gross elements. They contain truths and abilities beyond their physical expression that we as conscious beings can appreciate, use, and enjoy. Ayurveda has placed great value on the classification and study of these metaphysical qualities within the elements. This has given us psychological and emotional properties associated with each element, along with the physical traits we are all familiar with.

In order to move forward in our understanding of how the elements and their behaviors make it to not only our gardens but also our dinner tables, we must look at this through the lens of Ayurveda. To the present day, not many other spiritual or dietary sciences compare to Ayurveda's ability to inclusively bring it all together. As you will see as we go along, Ayurveda connects the elements to everything—most importantly, our sense of taste. This is how food can be used as medicine.

We will go further into this concept, but for now, simply understand that each taste we process from our food is also a way for consciousness to input the energy of the elements. In other words, when you identify a food's taste, it is your consciousness recognizing the information and energy encoded within that food. Taste is simply the enjoyment of that encoded information and energy. This can be understood and used for our well-being with a little wisdom regarding what the elements do and bring to our lives in their expression. The following is an outline of each of the five elements and how they can affect you and your loved ones when consumed.

>>>> SPACE <<<<

In Sanskrit, space, or ether, is known as *akasha*. As the first of the elements, it is thought to be what the entire universe is ultimately encased in. Since it is ephemeral and perpetually, eternally expansive, the true nature of ether is elusive to science. What Ayurveda tells us is that space correlates to all sound and the human organs that relate to sound, such as the ears and the vocal cords. Also relevant is the fact that all spaces, cavities, or openings in the body are indicative of the element of space within the human body.

>>>> AIR <<<<

All living beings on this planet are indebted to the element of air. *Vayu*, as it is known in Sanskrit, is considered the animating force behind all life. Space is the most necessary and primary element, but it is the movement within that space, air, that conducts most of the experience of life. In Ayurveda, vayu is literally present in everything that moves. Also, prana is derived from air, and we already covered the importance of prana to life. While it can be considered a specific aspect or manifestation of the air element, prana is the life force behind everything with consciousness. This connection alone supports the idea of air's importance to us all.

Aside from prana, air is responsible for the interaction of the other elements. It is the carrier and connector of all the elements that make up the universe. As such, Ayurveda connects air to all bodily move-ments, even down to the pulsation of your cells. Circulation within the bloodstream, the activity of the nervous system, the beating of your heart—literally all movement involves vayu. Ayurveda teaches us that air is most related to our sense of touch and our skin, of all things. This makes sense when it is seen that your skin is the primary way that you perceive air. Air is felt. In this way, it is always connected to wind.

✺✺✺ FIRE ✺✺✺

Fire, like air, is one of the more complex elements, because it is so dynamic and present within the world. This is evident in Ayurveda's treatment of and perspective on fire. Sanskrit gives the element of fire two commonly interchangeable yet different names, calling it *tejas* and *agni*. Most often, you will see *tejas* used when describing the light-bearing or illuminating characteristics of fire and *agni* used when speaking of its metabolic and transformational actions. However, this is not an absolute truth. They are, for the most part, interchangeable terms for this element.

For most purposes, especially those related to the body, fire is spoken of as agni. In Ayurvedic thought, agni is believed to be present in everything that is transformational or digestive. The human body has many forms of agni, and it is considered vital to all life processes. As life is constantly changing, the element of fire is always present. Fire is responsible for all our metabolic processes, not just food digestion. Ayurveda teaches that our eyes, brain, and cells also possess fire. It is present as the intelligence that digests input of data and sensory impressions from the outside world. It is not just fire in the sense of burning things, but light itself, including the light of consciousness. In this way, fire is connected to the Sun and intelligence very intimately. Ayurveda links fire to our ability to perceive, think, digest, process emotions, and metabolize nutrients. In this way, it is fundamental to our health and highly revered in Ayurveda.

>>>>> WATER <<<<<

Like fire, water is transformational, but in a different way. Water is responsible for binding and mixing. It is also necessary for life to occur. Within the body, water is present as everything that is fluid. Cytoplasm inside our cells, cerebrospinal fluid, plasma, mucus, saliva, body waste—all are linked to the element of water.

Since roughly 70 percent of our bodies, and of the planet's surface, is made of water, one can see its importance. Water is the nourishing principle of the universe, indicated by the fact that all life is dependent on it. One of its most important functions within Ayurveda is that it gives rise to our sense of taste. In this way, water (called *jala* in Sanskrit) is linked to the tongue, and obviously, a healthy, functioning tongue must maintain moisture. In a uniquely Ayurvedic way, water is also linked to procreation and the genitals. As the nourishing juices of biological life, water is present for us from the very beginning, and this relationship with water continues in the embryonic fluid.

Even after we leave the womb, moisture in the air is necessary so that there may be rain and cohesion of chemicals that sustain life. Water encases everything on the globe. As stated in the Bible, "Then God said, 'Let there be an expanse in the midst of the waters, and let it separate the waters from the waters.'"[65] Clearly, humanity, either consciously or unconsciously, acknowledges water for the blessing that it is. Without water, there is not life. So physiologically, water is of the utmost importance.

>>>>> EARTH <<<<<

Last, we arrive at earth. This element is responsible for all solidity and structure. This applies to the body in the form of bones, muscles, cartilage, and so on, and in nature, it is present as the literal earth or soil, rocks, and mountains. Basically, anything solid is attributed to earth.

In some ways, earth is considered the least of the five elements, because it is the most gross, dense form of matter. Matter itself

---

65 Biblica, Gen. 1:6.

is derived from earth. However, to say this doesn't place a lesser qualitative value on earth by any means. It is just to say that the universe has less matter than any of the other elements. It is the slowest, lowest vibrational form of energy. As modern science is discovering, all the matter in the universe combined makes up only about 5 percent or less of what the universe actually is. Our cutting-edge discovery of dark energy and matter in the universe is supporting information the Ayurvedic sages told us eons ago. This is what is meant by saying that it is the lesser of the elements. With that said, though, earth provides structure to everything in existence. Obviously, earth is also extremely important to plant life, as it is necessary for most plants to grow. Ayurveda connects earth to our sense of smell and the nose—and, almost humorously, to excrement.

When viewing the universal elements through this Ayurvedic lens, it is important to notice how this science works. Each element is understood to be more than its physical expression. Ayurveda uses our conscious experience of each element as a doorway into a deeper understanding of life in general. This is why when we speak of the elements, we link their attributes to specific body parts and functions. This is the Ayurvedic way.

This understanding comes from seeing the human being as a microcosmic expression of the universe. If these five elements are present in the universe at large, they are present within every level of the human being, meaning that there is a physical, psychological, and spiritual expression of each element. Therefore, each element is connected to body parts, emotions, and functions you may have never considered before.

To explore and apply Ayurveda in your garden, it is not necessary that you understand all the implications of the science and its treatment of the elements. The most important takeaways from this philosophy are that

- the five elements are present everywhere, including within yourself;
- the elements have specific qualities and energy that can be understood for better health and well-being;
- they are all interconnected and interdependent;
- the qualitative aspects of the elements are related to your consciousness and how you experience the world; and
- all the elements ultimately come from consciousness.

Aside from the individual character of each element, Ayurveda takes account of their behavior. The ancient sages made note of the fact that certain elements have a natural affinity for each other and are normally found interacting together in nature. This gives rise to what is known in Ayurveda as doshic theory. *Dosha* is another one of those slippery Sanskrit terms, because its English translations are "impurity" or "mistake." The term is used to indicate a kind of imbalance of the elements that is caused by the prevalence of certain elements over the others.

Keep in mind that all five elements are thought to be present in everything, but there are always two that seem to team together to express more powerfully or abundantly than the other three. In nature's infinite wisdom, these imbalances still seem to even out. However, as human beings with free will, we can sometimes behave and eat in ways that create imbalances within the body and/or mind. These imbalances are responsible for the experiences of disease and despair in our lives.

Ayurveda teaches us that the doshas come in three *tridoshas*, or recognizable pairings. These groupings are also always present together in each aspect of experience, but in pairs, they take on different functions. The tridoshas are as follows:

- **Vata:** space and air
- **Pitta:** fire and water
- **Kapha:** water and earth

The Sanskrit terms *vata*, *pitta*, and *kapha* do not have any adequate translations into the English language, but understanding that they refer to these elemental pairings is sufficient. By grouping together in these ways, the doshas express certain characteristics the individual elements do not fully do on their own.

Essentially, vata harnesses the universal energy of movement, pitta does so for transformation, and kapha expresses lubrication and structure. The key understanding of these doshas is that they act as the blueprint for how the elements behave within the microcosm of the body as well as within the macrocosm of the universe. If you consider that life's activity requires these three features—movement, transformation, and structure—the whole picture becomes clear. Whether a thing is active or still, conscious or not, there is some form of each of these qualities present. There is a scale for each doshic identifier that everything falls on.

For instance, while a human being and a rock may seem to have nothing in common, they both share the presence of the doshas. For the human, vata and pitta may be more relevant, whereas for the stone, kapha is its chief principle. Yet the human has kapha's solidity and structure, and the rock has pitta's transformation, albeit slow. Using the rock as a further example, its lack of vata, or movement, is compensated for in its extreme expression of kapha.

The doshas balance each other wherever they are found. It is not the kind of balance that one may be accustomed to, but there is always compensation of one or two of the three where the other is lacking. As stated, for living beings, this compensation can sometimes progress to disease, as the balance is delicate. However, what we are here to discuss are the positive benefits of recognizing this balance, working with it, and using the garden and our diets to create our best self. Nature is the absolute best example of what this balance should look like. As we have explored already, often, just being with nature is balancing in and of itself. Therefore, your garden can be a gateway for experiencing this balanced version of life.

Ayurveda teaches us repeatedly that the human being is a microcosm of this great universe, internally and externally. All the same elements are there, consciousness is present, and there really is not a separation. We only perceive and believe that we are separate. This belief leads to decisions and actions that are not always in our best interests. But with a little information and genuine intention, any person can achieve the necessary balance.

One of the first steps toward finding your own balance is understanding yourself as a manifestation of the doshas. Ayurveda offers us several means to do so, but one of the most effective and accessible is taking a dosha quiz. A quick online search will turn up numerous versions of the dosha quiz. There are slight differences in all of them, but each should have certain minimal descriptors. A good dosha quiz will ask you questions pertaining to your mental and physical attributes. It will also ask questions that apply to how you behave and react to life. The answers that you provide will identify you with certain qualities that are connected to specific elements and their character. From this examination, your dosha composition can be revealed. Other means such as pulse reading, visual analysis, and in-person interviewing can be used by a knowledgeable Ayurvedic professional. However, anyone can use the dosha quiz, so it is normally the most direct means. If you answer to the best of your ability and the quiz is accurate, your results should accurately capture your elemental makeup.

The quiz provided here is a two-part analysis, consisting of a prakriti quiz and one for vikriti. *Prakriti* is a Sanskrit word for the doshic composition that you were born with. In an Ayurvedic examination, the professional would take this result and compare it to the vikriti result, using these to find ways to align the two. *Vikriti* means the current dosha situation. This will be the most relevant to your routine gardening and diet. The reason for this is that once you know your primary doshic balance, the vikriti results can be used to see where and how you are out of synch with your true nature. For example, if you find that you are a kapha person, but your vikriti result reveals that currently you are in a vata mode, you would take the necessary steps in diet and routine to bring yourself back to the kapha spectrum. This will make more sense as we go along. Just know that as the elements are constantly in flux and motion in the natural world, they are also behaving this way within your body and mind. At this point, stop and take the dosha quizzes. Don't be concerned with the meanings or implications of the results just yet, as they will become clearer with more information.

⋙⋙ PRAKRITI QUIZ ⋘⋘

Instructions: Rank each characteristic as 3, 2, or 1 (3= most like me, 1 = least like me). Each row should have either a 3, 2, or 1 in every box totaling 6. Add up each dosha column at the bottom.

Characteristic	Vata	Pitta	Kapha
Eyes	I have small, darting eyes.	My eyes are clear and piercing.	I have large, round, sweet eyes.
Hair	My hair is dry and frizzy.	My hair is thin and/or graying.	I have thick, oily, and luscious hair.
Skin	My skin is dry, rough, and/or pale.	My skin is reddish, warm, and gets irritated easily.	My skin is thick, moist, and darker hued.
Frame	I am thin and light. My joints are visible.	I have a medium build and I'm naturally well toned.	I have a stocky build and rounded frame.
Temperament	I am an upbeat person and I'm always game for adventure.	I can be intense when I am focused on a goal.	I enjoy people and I'm generally easygoing.
Weight	I lose weight easily and work to keep it on.	I can will my body to lose or gain as I feel if I'm motivated.	I gain weight easily and have to work hard to lose it.
Sleep	I sleep lightly and rarely get a full night's rest.	I usually feel rested after 5-6 hours of sound sleep.	I sleep deeply and I'm always groggy when I first wake up.
Temperature	I get cold easily even when others are not.	I tend to feel hot most of the time and sweat easily.	I can do most weather but I'm not a big fan of rainy days.
Joints	My joints are bony and defined. My knuckles crack.	I never have problems; my joints are pretty flexible.	My joints are well padded, insulated, and round.
Stressed Out	I get anxious under pressure.	I'm mean when I'm under pressure, but I accomplish my goals.	I don't deal with stress well. I avoid it as much as I can.
Total	Vata Total:	Pitta Total:	Kapha Total:

VIKRITI QUIZ

Mind (Vata)	3, 2, or 1
My mind has been feeling cloudy lately.	
I feel like I'm all over the place.	
I haven't been sleeping well.	
I've been feeling restless.	
It's been really hard to focus on anything.	
Body (Vata)	
My skin has been really dry.	
I feel bloated on a regular basis.	
My hands and feet are always cold.	
My appetite is very sporadic.	
I experience chronic pain.	

Vata Mind Score:	Vata Body Score:

Mind (Pitta)	3, 2, or 1
I've been getting irritated very easily.	
I feel unsatisfied with my life right now.	
Other people frustrate me.	
I am strongly opinionated.	
I feel like I may snap at someone.	
Body (Pitta)	
I get heartburn regularly.	
My eyes get itchy and watery often.	
I've been having more bowel movements than normal.	
I get overheated easily.	
I have a really strong appetite.	

Pitta Mind Score:	Pitta Body Score:

Mind (Kapha)	3, 2, or 1
Food is my therapy when I'm feeling depressed.	
It's hard for me to get motivated in the morning.	
My life is cluttered lately.	
I've been wanting to change some of my bad habits, but I can't.	
There are things in my past that I just can't seem to leave behind.	
Body (Kapha)	
I am always sleepy after I eat.	
I regularly experience congestion in my head and chest.	
I feel heavy.	
I'm always sluggish in the morning.	
I sleep really hard for long periods of time.	

Kapha Mind Score:	Kapha Body Score:

CHARACTERISTICS OF THE DOSHAS

The following are some recognizable qualities human beings display as a result of the elemental composition within each of us. Once you are familiar with these concepts, you will be able to see their truth on full display not only in other people but also in your pets, in natural phenomena, and in worldly activities.

VATA

As stated, vata, being composed mostly of air and space, is responsible for movement. This shows itself in a person's personality, making one generally creative, talkative, always seeking new experiences, quick, easily distractible, flighty, irregular in routine, fast-speaking, unpredictable, and anxious. Vata people tend to be light and thin and to experience dry skin and hair more often than others. They are excitable and often show inconsistencies in their behavior.

Keep in mind that each of the doshas has an in-balance set of qualities and out-of-balance tendencies. For example, when in balance, vata is creative, communicative, energetic, lighthearted, and flexible. When out of balance, vatas experience insomnia, restlessness, poor digestion, anxiety, depression, extreme skin dryness, and emotional sensitivity.

➤➤➤➤ PITTA ◀◀◀◀

This dosha is mainly fire and water and corresponds to the universal principles of transformation and metabolism. That is why fire is the best overall metaphor for pitta. Like fire, it consumes and breaks down everything that it encounters. It is also fueled by matter and provides energy by transforming that matter into pure light and heat. As we have already discussed, Ayurveda treats fire as both tejas for its illuminating quality and agni for its heating, transformational characteristics. These same aspects of fire weigh heavily in the dosha fusion that is pitta.

Often, pitta is described by its fire principle, but one must also consider its water component. Like fire, water breaks material down and through this process creates transformation. However, water also provides the solution for enzymatic and chemical reactions. In human beings, pitta gives rise to a range of mental and physical characteristics. Pittas are highly intelligent, analytical, great leaders, visionaries, and good orators, and are generally strong personalities. They tend to be more materialistic, ambitious, and success driven. Physically, pittas have strong, steady digestion and warmer body temperatures, as well as medium builds and muscle tones. When in balance, pittas have a large capacity for learning, and they are intelligent and principled. An out-of-balance pitta, however, is overly critical of others, harsh, fanatical, prone to anger, jealous, and judgmental. Again, referring to the properties of fire, one can think of a pitta as a fiery personality, for all its positives and negatives.

⋙⋙ KAPHA ⋘⋘

Being mostly made of earth and water, the kapha dosha is everything that you would commonly attribute to these elements. Kapha is heavy, cold, sturdy, sticky, hard, and gross. Kapha is also responsible for lubrication, protection, structure, and steadiness. Kapha can be seen in everything from our bones and teeth to sinuses, joints, and hair. The physical body, itself, is largely produced by kapha. If you simply think about the characteristics of stone and earth, you can comprehend how these natural elements can be present within your mind and body.

Because of the nourishing effects of both water and earth, kapha people are normally nurturing, sweet-natured, caring, compassionate, and loving. They also display resilience, resolve, and steadfastness when facing life's challenges. They are not quick to action but are very determined—and unshakable once a course of action is chosen. Physically, kaphas tend to be larger people, sometimes tending toward obesity. Kaphas normally have round features, as well as oily, soft skin and thick, curly hair. Kaphas typically have a good, steady pace about themselves and excellent stamina. In balance, kaphas are friendly, giving, kind, and slow to anger. Out of balance, however, kaphas can be clingy, needy, lazy, and stubborn.

Now that we know a little more about how the doshas appear in humanity, you may be able to see more clearly how you can be classified as one of these doshas and recognize these qualities in others. Additionally, many people may find that they possess characteristics of two or more doshas. It is quite common to find that you are bidoshic, which occurs when you have scores coming in at a close second to your primary dosha.

For instance, a person may be vata pitta, meaning one is mostly vata but also has strong tendencies toward pitta. This often happens due to one dosha being more present in the mind, while the other is characterized in the body, or vice versa. This is not a problem in itself but can challenge you with another layer of consideration while you seek to balance your health. In very rare instances, we find those who are tridoshic, which means all three doshas are equally present in an individual. Tridoshic diagnosis can be complicated to balance when disease occurs but generally is benign when in balance. In fact, some may say that it allows for more flexibility, although it can also be a more sensitive balance to maintain.

Balance in general is not easy. However, Ayurveda has given us the tools to understand this balance and how these doshas play off one another. One simple rule of achieving doshic balance is to remember that like increases like and opposites reduce. When you are observing the elemental play of life, you can apply this logic to literally everything. Just as these elements have affinities we call doshas, they also have natural opposites based on their qualities. The following are the opposing relationships among the elements:

- ❀ **Vata:** space and air | **kapha:** water and earth
- ❀ **Pitta:** fire and water | **kapha:** water and earth
- ❀ **Kapha:** water and earth | **vata** and **pitta**

There are circumstances when certain specific qualities of a dosha may appear to balance in one direction yet increase in others. For instance, the space element in vata should technically bring balance to pitta's fire by giving it room to fizzle out. However, the air element and its moving-wind qualities can actually aggravate and invigorate pitta as well. Think about these elements literally as you encounter them, and this will easily make sense. The simplicity of Ayurveda is actually a testament to its brilliance!

One can also look at the relationship of kapha and pitta. They both have the element water. Logically, one may think that they would increase each other based on this, but the warming, invigorating fire of pitta, instead, balances the stagnant earth and water of kapha. In order to understand this better, we will now take a deeper look into the characteristics of each dosha.

The following are the attributes of each dosha. These are qualities that are indicative of the doshas as they show up in our physical and mental makeup. You may notice that the doshas that share certain elements also share certain attributes. For instance, because of their shared water element, kapha and pitta display an oily quality. Do not be thrown off by this. Just understand that when you see these characteristics shown in yourself or nature, they are clueing us in to the nature of the object in which they are presenting themselves.

VATA

- Dry
- Light
- Cold
- Rough
- Subtle
- Mobile
- Clear

PITTA

- Hot
- Sharp
- Light
- Liquid
- Spreading
- Oily
- Fleshy smell

KAPHA

- Heavy
- Slow
- Dull
- Cold
- Oily
- Liquid
- Slimy
- Smooth
- Dense
- Soft
- Static
- Sticky
- Cloudy
- Hard
- Gross

At this point, you may be saying to yourself, "This is great information, but what does this have to do with gardening?" The answer can be found in the application of this information to how we select and interact with the plants and produce of our gardens. Knowing your own personal elemental makeup allows you to choose which foods you need for balance. Also, it points the way to which gardening practices will be the most beneficial. You may recall from earlier chapters, specifically chapters 5, 6, and 7, how we can do certain activities in the garden to get more aligned with our plants. While these activities have their own merits, they can also be applied more acutely to balancing your health.

For example, a person experiencing a vata imbalance can use the practice of grounding in the garden to even out the excess air and space in the person's life with some earth. One can also spend extra meditation time in the garden for its calming effects, which will still the winds of one's mind. Another example is that a kapha person can use extra time and concentration on working in the garden in order to balance the stagnation and weight-gaining qualities of earth with a little processing power of fire.

Most significantly, this information can be applied to our diets. One of the reasons Ayurveda can be considered an effective way to bring spirituality to gardening and further promote this awakening in our daily lives is that it bridges our understanding of how our physical behaviors—eating, in particular—can affect us on deeper levels. To this point, Ayurveda emphasizes the importance of tastes and how they connect to these elements. Through this elemental connection, the things we eat can literally balance or unbalance our experience of the world at large.

Now that you understand your personal elemental composition as well as the Ayurvedic rule of like increases like and opposites reduce, we can explore the application of this knowledge. First, let's take a look at the way Ayurveda classifies the tastes and information we receive from our foods. Ayurveda considers all foods to fall into one or more of six taste categories: sweet, sour, salty, pungent (spicy), bitter, and astringent. These tastes our consciousness registers are considered the recognition of the elemental composition of the food. Here are the six tastes listed with their corresponding elements:

- **Sweet:** water and earth
- **Sour:** fire and earth
- **Salty:** fire and water
- **Pungent:** air and fire
- **Bitter:** space and air
- **Astringent:** air and earth

Unless you are already familiar with Ayurveda, this elemental view may seem like a foreign concept when applied to food and tastes. However, this view is simple and remarkably effective, as it has been medicinal for many people over the last 5,000 years.

Using one's food as medicine can be a very real tool toward your healing and well-being. Let's explore some of the possible scenarios in which this could come in handy. For instance, a vata imbalance, characterized by an excess of space and air, can be balanced by sweet-, sour-, or salty-tasting food because those tastes are not dominated by air or space. Also, the elements they contain are balancing to space and air, the most effective of which is sweet, because both water and earth dissipate air and space when in contact with them.

This is how each taste matches up to each dosha:

- **Vata:** increased by pungent, bitter, and astringent; balanced by sweet, sour, and salty
- **Pitta:** increased by sour, salty, and pungent; balanced by sweet, bitter, and astringent
- **Kapha:** increased by sweet, sour, and salty; balanced by pungent, bitter, and astringent

By being aware of this, as well as our doshic compositions, one can plan one's meals around what is needed in one's life on a deeper level as easily as one follows one's cravings. You may already do this based on habit, family tradition, or craving and not be aware of it. All Ayurveda is doing is making you a more conscious choice maker and therefore a healthier individual. Examples of this are eating spicy (pungent) foods while experiencing sinus congestion (kapha) or enjoying cucumbers and watermelon for their cooling water properties during the heat of summer.

If you really analyze your diet, especially those foods and herbs traditionally passed down from older generations, you'll see that this Ayurvedic concept of food as medicine is not as foreign as it may seem. Ayurveda makes a science of it and arms us with the information to fully utilize our foods. As the grower of your own foods in the garden, you can pick and choose those that provide the most healing to you and your family. By knowing your doshic qualities, you can turn your garden into its own kind of pharmacy. For instance, if you and your family are mostly kapha inclined, planting spicy, invigorating foods in your garden for you all to routinely mix into your diet can help balance the household. Also, on a visual level, your landscaping can feature a more vibrant coloration through the flowers you choose and cultivate. These colors also have effects on the doshas, as do the aromas of these plants.

To further our understanding, here is a listing of some of the commonly grown garden foods and their Ayurvedic classifications:

VATA-PACIFYING FOODS

- Asparagus
- Beets
- Turnips
- Onions (cooked)
- Garlic (cooked)
- Carrots
- Cucumbers
- Okra
- Sweet potatoes

- Radishes
- Bananas
- Apricots
- Melons
- Oranges
- Papayas
- Rice
- Coconut
- Berries

- Avocado
- Pineapple
- Plums
- Cherries
- Grapes
- Nectarines
- Oats
- Wheat
- Peaches

You may notice that many of the foods on this list are root vegetables. Using our newly acquired Ayurvedic understanding of the elements and their qualities, this should make sense. Vata, being mostly  space and air, should naturally be balanced by those foods that are nearest to the earth and that contain the characteristics of grounding and calming. Also, many of the fruits and grains on this list have a characteristic sweetness, which is also grounding, as the taste of sweet indicates the presence of water and earth. In general, juicy, well-ripened fruit will be calming to vata.

VATA-AGGRAVATING FOODS

- Leafy greens
- Peas
- Potatoes
- Sprouts
- Zucchini
- Broccoli
- Brussel sprouts
- Cabbage
- Cauliflower
- Celery
- Mushrooms
- Peppers
- Sprouts
- Corn
- Barley
- Pomegranates
- Cranberries
- Apples
- Buckwheat
- Dry oats
- Rye
- Pears
- Nuts

While some of these are also root vegetables, the difference is that they contain the elements space, air, or fire. While this may not be apparent from the food itself, one can look to their tastes as a guide. Remember, vata is increased by the tastes pungent, bitter, and astringent. This can be rectified by cooking the vegetables and making them extra oily. The oil adds qualities that balance the dryness of these foods in their raw form. The dry, rough, and acidic qualities of these foods contribute to their vata-increasing quality. Also, unripe fruit increases vata.

PITTA-PACIFYING FOODS

- Sweet peppers
- Okra
- Peas
- Leafy greens
- Lettuce
- Celery
- Asparagus
- Cabbage
- Sprouts
- Coconut
- Grapes
- Sweet potatoes
- Cauliflower
- Zucchini
- Melons
- Apples
- Mangoes
- Figs
- Oranges
- Brussels sprouts
- Raisins
- White rice
- Pears
- Plums
- Wheat
- Barley
- Cherries
- Sunflower seeds
- Pumpkin seeds
- Cucumbers

Pitta is calmed by foods that are sweet, bitter, and astringent. Also, foods that are cooling or juicy are balancing to pitta's fire element. With practice, keeping the elemental quality of both the food and your doshas in mind will make a lot of this seem like common sense to you.

PITTA-AGGRAVATING FOODS

- Hot peppers
- Grapefruit
- Lemons
- Onions
- Radishes
- Tomatoes
- Sour cherries
- Corn
- Brown rice
- Garlic
- Apricots
- Sour fruit

The key thing to remember in order to not increase pitta is to avoid foods that have the fire element in them. This includes foods that taste sour, salty, and, of course, pungent (spicy). Also, when experiencing a pitta imbalance, it is best to avoid piping-hot food. Instead, go for warm or even cool prepped foods.

KAPHA-PACIFYING FOODS

- Most vegetables
- Apples
- Cranberries
- Pears
- Most dried fruits
- Pomegranates
- Mushrooms
- Barley
- Corn
- Rye
- Pumpkin seeds
- Sunflower seeds
- Legumes

As kapha dosha is made of stagnant, slow-moving water and earth, the balancing factors are those that stir it up and cause movement. Chiefly, fire and air (wind) balance kapha. Therefore, foods with pungent, bitter, and astringent tastes are used for fixing kapha imbalances.

KAPHA-AGGRAVATING FOODS

- Avocados
- Mangoes
- Tomatoes
- Sweet potatoes
- Melons
- Zucchini
- Bananas
- Peaches
- Coconuts
- Dates
- Pineapples
- Rice
- Oats

In general, foods are not necessarily the problem for kapha people. Food choices can be detrimental, but the individual foods themselves are not. The real issue in many kaphas is lack of movement and exercise to use the energy of their foods and burn calories. As kaphas have a natural tendency toward weight gain, it is more important to get moving and be active.

The foods listed above may increase kapha, due to their water content and sweet tastes. Remember, like increases like. Adding more water or juiciness to a dosha that consists of water will only add to the imbalance. Also, sweet consists of exactly the elements of kapha dosha: water and earth. Therefore, eating sweet-tasting foods is akin to eating bits of kapha. In moderation, this is not a problem. However, most people in modern Western society consume way more sugar than they should to maintain optimal health. Sugars are found in almost everything fast, processed, or packaged.

As a result, many are getting an excess of this taste already, even in foods that are not sugary and in popular drinks, then adding sweet foods to their diet to boot. If you add the high salt content of many foods to the equation, with their water-retaining qualities, it becomes obvious why kapha imbalances are so common today.

A natural kapha may be a bigger person organically. However, when in balance, this kapha will show in all the positive characteristics and good health, not sickness or extreme obesity. Being naturally bigger is one thing, but it should not affect one's general health. When a person shows signs of ill health, Ayurveda always credits this to a dosha imbalance. So, when we speak of the weight gain caused by kapha dosha, that is not to say anything negative about a person's size. Rather, it speaks of the excessive unnecessary fat or water content that can cause problems within the body. An active, healthy kapha can be heavier-set yet noticeably more vibrant, strong, and energetic than an unhealthy counterpart.[66]

Let us also consider our herbs and how they can be used medicinally to offset our dosha imbalances. You may find yourself unable or unwilling to always adhere strictly to those foods that balance your dosha. This is normal and completely fine. In fact, Ayurveda highly recommends a variety of tastes and colors in our daily intake of food. The information provided thus far is not meant to be a strict guideline for how we should eat. Much like the doshas themselves, our diets should include all the elements.

However, just as the doshas show an abundance of the particular elements that give them their recognizable character, you should have a little more of those foods that are most balancing. Of course, this is not always possible. As a remedy to these detours from your dosha-pacifying food groups, you can always incorporate herbs and spices. This helps, especially in times when you are sharing a meal with others. Rather than catering everything to your personal needs, you can eat whatever is present

---

66 Deepak Chopra, *Perfect Health: The Complete Mind/Body Guide*, revised ed. (London: Bantam, 2001).

and add these herbs to your plate as a way of still getting the medicinal value of conscious eating.

Most of these herbs are easily grown in the garden or even within the home, and they provide great medicine for a variety of things. Here is a doshic breakdown of some common garden herbs that you may already grow or be familiar with:

VATA-PACIFYING HERBS/SPICES

- Basil
- Cardamom
- Ginger
- Marjoram
- Nutmeg
- Bay leaves
- Black pepper

PITTA-PACIFYING HERBS/SPICES

- Lemongrass
- Coriander
- Cilantro
- Mint
- Fennel
- Cumin
- Dill
- Licorice

KAPHA-PACIFYING HERBS/SPICES

- Cayenne
- Cinnamon
- Basil
- Ginger
- Mustard
- Parsley
- Sage
- Black pepper
- Rosemary
- Fenugreek[67]

Now, armed with all this Ayurvedic information, we can cultivate our gardening into more than just a nice pastime. It may seem like a lot to think about at first, but after applying this knowledge for a season or two, it will become a natural way to garden for you. Building an Ayurveda-inspired routine into your gardening practice does not have to be so cerebral as reading and processing all this may seem. Let's look at some examples of what a full-scale spiritual gardening experience might look like. You may try these out as templates for what to do until you gain your bearings on the

---

[67] David Simon, *The Wisdom of Healing: A Natural Mind Body Program for Optimal Wellness* (New York: Harmony, 1997).

whole concept. Once you have a grasp of how this works, feel free to mix things up and see what works for you. Especially when considering your dosha balance, these practices will need to be routinely altered and tested for the highest efficacy. Also, you may find that other members of your household may have different needs for balance that can also be incorporated alongside your own. Here are some suggestions for pulling all this together:

VATAS

- Plot the garden based on vata-pacifying foods and herbs.
- Spend extra quiet reflection time in the garden.
- Focus on gratitude toward plants throughout the growing process.
- Emphasize connecting with plants on a consciousness level through deep, slow breathing with them during time in the garden.
- Make a routine of going out and talking to your plants.
- Practice grounding in the garden, especially during times of unrest or feeling overwhelmed.
- Meditate in the garden regularly. Specifically focus on the thought "Life and grace flow through me" and variants that align with this concept. Consciously seek to be in tune with the beauty and sensuality of your garden.

PITTAS

- Plot the garden based on pitta-pacifying foods and herbs.
- Avoid gardening during the heat of the day, preferably doing your work tasks early in the morning or in the evening before sunset.
- Make sure your garden has shaded areas to relax in and enjoy.
- Place energy into the design and layout of the garden and landscaping. Focus on its aesthetics just as much as, if not more than, its efficiency.
- Use the garden space for calm, quiet reflection time. Specifically, when you are angry or frustrated, go out into the garden and relax alongside your plants. Breathe with them and release your energy.

- Consciously seek connection with your plants during watering times. Water them and then sit with them, taking in the fresh smells and beauty of your garden.
- Routinely meditate in the garden, especially when there is a need for calm and quiet. Align with the thought "My attention is an agent of growth." See and live this truth through your gardening.
- Connect with the growth process of the garden from start to finish. See yourself and your influence on the lives of the plants.
- Appreciate the benefits, both mentally and in diet, you are receiving from your work and attention.

KAPHAS

- Plot the garden based on kapha-pacifying foods and herbs.
- Concentrate your efforts on maintenance and upkeep of your garden.
- More so than the other doshas, you can work in the garden during the heat of the day. With respect to your comfortability level, make a routine of doing this. Welcome the sweat, the heat, the sunshine.
- Keep an awareness of the need for weeding and clearing the garden of invasive plants. Do not procrastinate in taking care of these unwanted guests. Rather, use their removal as an opportunity for exercise and caring for your plants.
- Practice the sound-based therapies of chanting and tuning in your garden.
- Decorate your garden space with vibrant, invigorating colors and designs. Make use of bright tapestries or prayer flags as part of the garden layout.
- Meditate in the garden, specifically aligning with the thought "As I nourish, so am I nourished." Synch with the reality that you are gardening as a positive dietary choice, that your efforts to bless the plants will return to you in your food and health.

⟫⟫⟫ ONENESS WITH NATURE MEDITATION ⟪⟪⟪

By now, if you've been following along, you should be a lot more familiar with meditation. As we wind down our journey, the intention of this meditation is to give the inner experience of how all this applies to you personally. In the previous chapter, we covered several ways you are inherently connected to the universe. Now, let's meditate on these connections and how each of us relates to the cosmos.

Start by getting comfortably seated. If you prefer, this meditation can be enhanced by experiencing it outdoors while in or around your garden. Begin with some deep belly breaths to clear your mind. Gently squeeze your diaphragm so that all the air leaves your body. On your next inhalation, relax and release your abdomen slowly, allowing the air to pour back into your lungs without effort. Once you have gotten comfortable with this, give yourself about seven breath cycles.

This meditation can be done with your eyes open or closed—whichever feels the most calming to you in this moment. If you are closing your eyes, do so now as you come to the end of the seven breaths. Continue to breathe in this way while remaining still and relaxed. Allow your mind to wander, but pull back from the chatter in detachment. Simply observe your thoughts without engaging in them or giving them too much energy. Stay centered and focused on the breath.

Give yourself about three more deep belly breaths, but now, intentionally become aware of how the breath feels as it enters your body. Feel the air enter your nose. Visualize its path as it travels up, passes your brain, goes down into your chest, and fills your entire inner space with sensation. Exhale with this same visual of the air coming up through your body, passing your heart, and going into your head and back out through your nose. Become one with this breath by focusing all your attention on it. Notice how its rhythm sets the pace and energy of your whole being. As it flows, your blood circulation reacts, your mind reacts, your body temperature reacts—all over, your body synchs to this ebb and flow of prana.

Remember that this prana is the life breath of the universe, the carrier of consciousness within every living thing. Feel it move through you. Become aware of how it leaves your body and fills the space around you. Exhale, and visualize it expanding out away from you, disappearing into the air like smoke, filtered into the atmosphere. Recall the way the breath felt in your body, how it moved and affected everything within you. That breath now joins with nature and moves and affects something. Your plants are nourished by it as it swirls into a mix of the outdoor winds. They breathe it in, it flows into their cells, they are enlivened.

Stay with your breathing pace. Exhale fully as if you want to push that breath out to the horizon. Listen to its flow. Now relax, knowing that it returns to you without effort or exertion—freely, as a loving support to your life. Free your mind of outside thoughts and focus on this movement for a few moments. The energy goes into you, then out into the world. Out of the world, and into you. This is and has been going on all the time, since the first moments of your life. Always present. Always flowing. We are merely paying attention to it. Watching, appreciating.

This prana, this life, is you. It has always been a part of you. It moves throughout everything that is. And everything that is abundantly gives it back, each one taking in its own little bit of it. Life, energy, carrier of consciousness. Animator of the entire universe. Take three deep breaths with attention to these words. Allow your mind to freely digest them. Do not engage with the thoughts. Visualize even the thoughts as dust particles and droplets in the mix of breath you share with the world. Moving through you, moving the world around you. Touching each element, giving life to them all. Shared by all, in harmony. Your plants feel what you feel in their own unique way. Their inner spaces bathed by the inhalation. The sensation of offering it back into the world.

Contemplate this unity for a few more breaths. Pay attention to how it feels and where you feel it most. Focus completely on this breath, knowing that it is the universal mover of all life, the unifying factor between you and all life, you and your environment, life shared between you and your garden. Take two more deep breaths, and when it feels comfortable, open your eyes.

YOU ARE THE GARDEN

"A society grows great when old men plant trees whose
shade they know they shall never sit in."

—*Greek proverb*

From seed to harvest, with intention and care, you should now have
all you need to build a beautiful and fulfilling gardening experience.
Whether you are just starting out or you seek to enhance your current gardening practice, it has been the intention of this journey that
you will find greater depth of wisdom than you may have previously
thought possible. The garden has always been a special place for
humanity. Those who are aware of its secrets have found a value that
can be understood only through involvement. From the Garden of
Eden to your cozy home plot, there is a lineage of health, happiness,
nourishment, and wonder that only a few will ever know.

Authentic communion with nature and knowing of one's higher
self are possible. It is within the garden that the truths of the human
experience are unveiled, where humanity finds its rightful place in the
natural world—part caretaker, part enjoyer, sometimes at its mercy,
and sometimes its master. Humanity is just as much a part of this
amazing dance of life as it is an observer of it. Your garden can teach
you who you really are if you seek its wisdom. Believe it or not, this
understanding is accessible to you now.

You may take this information to merely be useful as an alternative agricultural teaching. But in truth, it is so much more. If you take what you have learned about the plants themselves and their consciousness, utilize the Ayurvedic practices, and spend some meaningful reflective time in your garden, you may be surprised at what you can discover. In reality, the garden is just as much a part of you as it is part of the natural world outside of you. All your effort, time, and consideration will produce more value for you than the food it gifts you with. It is in the journey, the sweat, the small miracles, the beauty, the tastes, and the aromas.

This is not said to romanticize the act of gardening with flowery language. It is a statement of truth that can be realized only by approaching your garden from a spiritual place within. In doing so, one can open up a spiritual place outside in the garden. A place of peace, calm and serenity. A place of healing and deep wisdom. A place of attunement between the heavens of your higher inner dimensions and the depths of the earth beneath your feet. The divine realms of reality and consciousness have always come to us through the garden. Just because we have grown accustomed to visiting the supermarket or ordering takeout doesn't mean we cannot still access this kind of mystical relationship with nature and the plant kingdom.

We have looked at the seeds of this relationship between humanity and nature. We have taken full stock of the modern situation and the potential that mindful gardening can help us reach in today's ecological and financial grounds. We have explored the ways in which we can water and grow a spiritual gardening practice with special care and nourishment. We have looked to the wisdom traditions of the past for enlightenment and truth. Now it is time to harvest the power of this knowledge by putting it to use and experiencing all that it has to offer us.

There is so much more that can be gained from this kind of gardening practice and insight, but the best of it will not be realized from reading about it in a book. One could write a whole series of books about this subject and still not come close to the wisdom in one special moment of realization reaped from the garden. You may find that your first experiences of gardening with this perspective won't hold any deeper significance or insights. Maybe you just get to have fun with it and try some new things to spice up your gardening hobby. This, too, in time will open you up to undiscovered possibilities if followed with intention and awareness.

Stay with it. Pay attention to it. Grow it. With time and grace, you will find there is much more going on in your garden than just some plants that you cultivate for food. There is a relationship. There is a realization. There is a potential for higher consciousness. Just as your food and behaviors shape who you are physically, now you should understand that with the right awareness they can have great effects on who you are mentally and spiritually. These are the true gifts of the garden: freedom, independence, connection, and realization.

No longer does gardening have to be just a hobby or something you do to supplement your food costs. It can be a gateway and a true delight. Remember that you are not only the gardener but also the experience of the garden itself. How you feel about your garden, how you perceive the process, and how you interact with it all contribute to the growth and even the nutrients you are able to reap from it.

If you don't gain anything else from this work, the intention is that you will come to see yourself as a more integrated part of the process of the garden from start to finish. That you will be able to place not only your physical labor into it but also aspects of your entire being. You select the land it will be plotted on. You decide which seeds are to be grown. You water and nourish the plants. You take care of the plants and ensure optimal growth conditions. You decorate it and accentuate it. You spend your time and energy in making it the best garden that it can be. You enjoy its sights and aromas. And ultimately, it is you who reaps its harvest for yourself and your loved ones.

In this way, your life energy and attention is mixed in with every aspect of the garden. Your consciousness and that of the plant life you cultivate are coalescing into a wonderful experience—one as old and organic as human life on this planet. You can continue to simply garden as you may have before, but hopefully, by reading this book, you are now open to the true power and importance of the act. The garden and all that grows within it are just as much a part of you as the cells of your body. In fact, they will literally become part of your body through the act of eating and experience. This is the gift of spiritual gardening. To become aware of this. To place your whole attention and consciousness into it.

And through this kind of practice and wisdom, you will grow. You will grow awesome, life-nourishing food. You will grow in insight and stability of well-being. You will grow in your ability to sustain and pass this knowledge on to future generations. You will grow as a citizen of the life of this planet. But most important, you will grow in consciousness.

⟫⟫⟫ CLOSING/HARVEST MEDITATION ⟪⟪⟪

Get comfortable. You may lie down or sit for this meditation, focusing only on stillness, stability, and centering. (If you would like to get the full experience, you are encouraged to do this meditation outside in your garden or in the presence of your indoor plants.) Close your eyes. Begin breathing deeply. Make these slow, full belly breaths, using the diaphragm to squeeze your exhalation out as fully as possible.

For this exercise, we will be intentionally squeezing all the air out that we can and gently releasing to slowly fill our lungs, forcefully exhaling out the nose, gently relaxing the diaphragm, and slowly, without force, drifting the inhalation back into your nose. This may seem difficult at first, so if it proves to be too much of a distraction, just focus on breathing deeply and relaxing more and more with every breath. Let's do seven of these cycles of constricting the diaphragm and breathing out forcefully. You may begin to notice a slight euphoria or lightness in the slow inhalation. Just maintain the breath and let it wash over you.

On the last exhalation, release your diaphragm and allow your body to breathe as it will. Stay here for a moment, just watching the sensations and movement of your body. Follow your breath flow in through your nostrils—feel it breeze over your brain and down into your chest. Notice any changes in breathing from before. Is your breathing shallow now? Is it still flowing deeply? Don't take control of it— just observe its rhythm. Let your thoughts drift while paying them no attention. Remain as a witness, and do not allow yourself to be carried away with anything you see or hear. No matter what the thought is, give it no energy. Do not resist it; do not enjoy it. Just let it pass.

Now, think of the first meditation we did together. How did you feel? What were you expecting? What did you experience? Do not try to consciously answer any questions right now. Just hear them and allow your mind to respond. Continue to breathe deeply and visualize the air as it enters and exits your body. Release any tension you feel with every exhalation. Relax your face and jaw; relax your shoulders. With every breath, go a little deeper.

Now, picture yourself doing the work. Imagine watching as you picked out plants, as you dug up the soil and placed them. Visualize their growth. Remember any exercises that you tried from this book. With detachment, watch as the whole journey unfolds. Take three deep breaths. Now, be in the present moment. See the events that led to now as you sit, centered. Know that everything that preceded right now is here with you. In every inhalation, you take in that which is present. With every exhalation you push out, a new event begins. Receiving and giving, seed and harvest in every moment, with every breath. Reflect on this for a few moments, engaging deeply with the simple act of breathing.

Now, let us introduce a sweet thought as our mantra. Within your silence, begin to say the words, "I harvest the fruits of my past. I sow the seeds of my future." If it helps, synchronize the words with your breath. Inhale "I harvest the fruits of my past." Exhale "I sow the seeds of my future." Say, "I harvest the fruits of my past. I sow the seeds of my future." Repeat this for seven slow, deep breaths. Afterward, just be still. Be right here, right now. Take a breath or two to recenter in the present moment.

As we close this meditation, turn in toward your heart center. If it helps, touch the center of your chest; feel your breath and pulse. With intention on your heart, say, "Thank you for my harvest." Do this three times with sincere gratitude for the blessings of your life and the blessing that you are to others. After you have said, "Thank you," you may release the meditation and slowly open your eyes.

MANDALA

An imprint of MandalaEarth
PO Box 3088 San Rafael, CA 94912
www.MandalaEarth.com

Find us on Facebook: www.Facebook.com/MandalaEarth
Follow us on twitter: @MandalaEarth

Text © 2022 Leo Carver

ISBN: 978-1-64722-420-2

PUBLISHER: Raoul Goff
ASSOCIATE PUBLISHER: Phillip Jones
VP OF CREATIVE: Chrissy Kwasnik
ASSOCIATE ART DIRECTOR: Ashley Quackenbush
DESIGNER: Amy DeGrote
EDITORIAL DIRECTOR: Katie Killebrew
EDITOR: Matt Wise
EDITORIAL ASSISTANT: Sophia Wright
SENIOR PRODUCTION MANAGER: Greg Steffen

 ROOTS of PEACE REPLANTED PAPER

Earth Aware Editions, in association with Roots of Peace, will plant two trees for
each tree used in the manufacturing of this book. Roots of Peace is an internationally
renowned humanitarian organization dedicated to eradicating land mines worldwide
and converting war-torn lands into productive farms and wildlife habitats. Roots of
Peace will plant two million fruit and nut trees in Afghanistan and provide farmers
there with the skills and support necessary for sustainable land use.

Manufactured in India by Insight Editions

10 9 8 7 6 5 4 3 2 1

FSC FSC® C010615
MIX
Paper